Executive Coach and former President of Trainline Intl

DANIEL BEUTLER

Exit Ahead

The Scale-Up Playbook

Cover image by: Enrico Fioraso
Book design by: SWATT Books Ltd

Printed in the United Kingdom
First Printing, 2021

ISBN: 978-3-9822962-0-3 (Paperback)
ISBN: 978-3-9822962-1-0 (eBook)

Daniel Beutler
23879 Mölln
Germany

www.danielbeutler.coach

Table of Contents

Dedication 5

About the Author 6

Preface 7

Section I: The Foundations **11**

Chapter 1: Before Take-Off Checklist 12

Chapter 2: The Early Scaler Catches the Exit 19

Chapter 3: Becoming a Corporate Athlete 30

Section II: The Scaling Phase...**41**

Chapter 4: People. People. People. 42

Chapter 5: The Role that has No Peers 63

Chapter 6: You're Not Building it for Yourself 84

Chapter 7: The One-Billion-Euro-Story 100

Section III: The Exit Preparation...**117**

Chapter 8: All On Green is Not On Track 118

Chapter 9: And Now, it's Really Time to Play 132

Appendix

Your Playbook Summary 152

Glossary...154

Bibliography 157

Dedication

To my son, who slept on me for the first months of his life while I wrote this book.

About the Author

Daniel is 39 years old, married and father of a little boy. Born and raised in Hamburg, Germany, he has lived and worked in many parts of the world, the last decade in Paris, before now moving back closer to his home town. After 5 years as a corporate CEO with Deutsche Bahn, a leading transportation company, he continued his career in the start-up world to become COO of Captain Train. Following their acquisition by Trainline, which he led in a transformational change process, he became President of Trainline Intl and a leader in creating one of the biggest European tech hits and IPOs of recent years.

Today, Daniel uses his experience to focus on executive business coaching and serves as advisor to leaders from the corporate world and from start-ups. He accompanies them on their journey to achieve their goals. Daniel is trilingual (English, French, German) and studied at McGill University in Montreal and Dresden University of Technology, holding a master's degree in Transport Economics and is a graduate of the Meyler Campbell Business Coaching Mastered programme.

in https://www.linkedin.com/in/dbeutler/
🐦 https://twitter.com/danielmbeutler/

Preface

There are not even 15 companies who become unicorns in Europe every year. Being part of this exclusive club now makes me feel privileged and humbled. I was fortunate enough to even exit our company twice in 3 years: our start-up (Captain Train) was acquired by Trainline and we concluded a successful IPO as a merged company just three years later. However, people may be dazzled by this outward show of progress, seeing just the tip of the iceberg and not the crazy amount of work, dedication and resilience it takes to arrive there. The latter is precisely what I'm going to focus on in this book – how to get the scale-up process right for both your business and for you personally.

My story starts with the scaling phase and describes how it can lead to a successful exit. It's written from a C-level perspective with a strong coaching influence and is aimed at everybody who wants to lead or get involved in a rapidly growing digital business. Whether you're a leader of a start-up with big ambitions, a potential investor in a scale-up or an intrapreneur in a corporate setting, this book is designed to help you to maximize your chances of creating a successful and prosperous exit. For all other curious folks out there, this is your opportunity to peak behind the scenes of a multibillion-euro success story.

Why am I writing this book?

Well, there are four reasons really:

The first one is that so often I would have loved to have a playbook like this – it would have saved me all that time that I spent making mistakes and losing focus on the important things. It would also have helped me to be able to measure whether we were on track towards success.

Secondly, during my times as an executive, as well as in coaching and board sessions, I have constantly been interrogated on my success recipe. This book is part of my attempt to answer to that question and in an altruistic way to put you in a better starting block than I was in back then.

Thirdly, I was lucky enough to be surrounded by people who supported me and shared invaluable pieces of advice during my journey. They made me promise to pass this on if I ever felt that it would help someone else, so I have tried to do that justice by writing this.

And, last but not least, there is a tangible monetary value to this exercise. If you create your own playbook correctly, it will significantly add to the valuation of your company. So, I hope this book can serve as a starting point to build out your very own playbook more easily and successfully.

This book is structured in chronological order, starting from the beginnings of a scale-up-to-exit journey right through to its successful conclusion. We start by answering all the appropriate questions needed to build a solid foundation before scaling up and preparing your exit. Along the way, you will see that there is a major people element at the core of this book, as I found that it is people that make this journey work, with tech and marketing only helping to serve the cause.

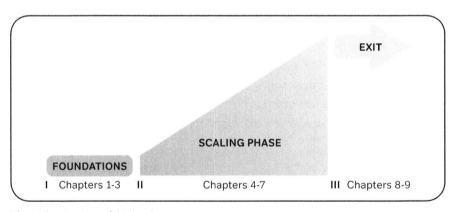

Fig 1: *The structure of this book*

At the end of each chapter, I summarize the three key takeaways, which I have tried to formulate in as practical terms as possible, creating a checklist for your own playbook, with then a complete overview at the end. I have also tried to make it as accessible as possible, remembering often feeling uneducated when reading these kinds of books or in meetings with abbreviations being slathered around. This book is designed to help you to learn enough about this topic so that you can come away feeling highly informed, and able to pass on its lessons to others. That's why I have also included a glossary of key abbreviations in the end, so that you can look up key terms and bring up your score for your next bullshit bingo round.

For half a decade I put all my heart and energy into the project I describe in this book to ensure it worked out. It's a proudly European project, played out in a business environment where successful exits are at a lower value and fewer in number than, for example, in the US. It's about a German who worked in France for a British-French company with some significant business in Italy. To this heady European mix, you will find that I have brought some management approaches influenced by my studies in Canada. As a result, this book is also about my appreciation for diverse cultures and values and the key role they have played in my professional success.

But it's also a personal and human story of making bold moves and building trust. The day of the announcement of the successful conclusion of our B-Series, the second fundraising round, was also the day I officially joined Captain Train. Jean-Daniel, its founder, summarized that moment beautifully: *"Daniel could have continued a promising career with Deutsche Bahn, which started 8 years ago, but no, he has decided to join this bunch of utopians who want to change the world pixel by pixel."* And that's how it all started, and boy, I never regretted that move.

Finally, this is also the story of all the amazing people I have had the pleasure and honour to work with – the believers and the haters – who both equally gave me the motivation to hang in there and succeed. And I owe a massive thank you to all of you great people in particular who gave me super helpful feedback on the content of this book – it wouldn't be the same without you: Carl, Delphine, Elise, Enrico, Hélène, Jean-Daniel, Lucile, Mark, Mounir, Neil, Nico, Sam and Silja.

SECTION I

The Foundations

CHAPTER 1

Before Take-Off Checklist

B efore we start talking about how to scale a company, I suggest **taking a step back, looking at the foundations** of any company first and whether they are solid enough to be scaled upon. Whether it's your company or one you are thinking of joining, this is a vital first step. Equally important is to check whether this is the right business for you personally. Either way, things are about to get tougher and more frenetic, and if your true passion is not in this business, then you will soon lose heart. Don't just fall for great storytelling – after all, most founders and executives have told their stories so many times that they are incredibly convincing. Instead, ask a set of key questions that can help you in your assessment.

Are you a founder or CEO? This is relevant to you too. It can't hurt to set yourself the challenge or discuss with your board to see if you can answer to your own satisfaction the questions that I lay out here. Either way, you will only want to make many personal sacrifices if you at least have a fair chance of being paid back royally in the end and the prospect of enjoying the most amazing ride.

Why am I insisting on conducting such a thorough evaluation before starting to scale? The start-up phase may be over, and decisions are being made on whether to take it to the next level with the injection of some significant investment. At this stage you need to ensure that this massive house you're trying to construct will not be built on shaky foundations. At this point, the risk is still great that the business may lose focus or you discover misalignments among key team members, which have the potential to cause frustration and even lead to the whole endeavour failing. You only have limited energy and resources available to succeed, and answering fundamental questions upfront will ensure a smoother ride during the scaling phase. Having said that, even then, with external factors lurking beyond our control, there cannot be given any guarantee that it will work out as planned. However, answering the following questions can ensure you find out the likely success of the project and evaluate your personal fit.

To evaluate the project's chances of success, a good starting point is to look at the company from a potential investor's point of view: would you trust this business with your money? From my experience of some hundred pitches on both the pitching and the receiving end, this breaks down to the following 5 categories of questions to check on:

1. Does the company's product solve a specific customer need? Is there a market?

2. How easily is the product/company replicable? What are market entrance barriers and competitors? How easy would it be for a huge incumbent to invest heavily in trying to copycat?

3. Can the playbook be rolled out easily to other geographic territories? Are there obvious limitations to growth?

4. If an extra million became available, what would the business invest in? What is the growth focus?

5. What is the goal of the company? Is there a plan to scale and an exit?

Now, you bought their story and double-checked it by asking your own questions, so why stop there? You can triple-check their story by conducting further research, bringing in **external sources**. Speak with people who have worked with the folks in question. Look at the market and its trends, search for rulings and regulations that potentially might stand in the way of growth, and undertake a benchmark on the competitors.

Even if, following all this research, you conclude that the company is scalable, this does not necessarily make it the right business for you. So, you should also check on your **personal fit**. Firstly, you need to believe that the management team, which you might be(come) a part of, is the right one to lead the project to an exit. And secondly, are your values and those of the team aligned to ensure you reach a successful conclusion? The following questions can help to check if there is a match in culture and expectation:

- What are the company's key values?
- Will you be able to add something to the company that they don't already have?
- What can your role evolve into in the future?
- Will the founders remain onboard? If so, do they get along well, are they aligned on the strategy and the timing to exit, and what will their roles be? Do they consider themselves capable of scaling the business or will they be looking for help?

And even if all these tests come back positive, still keep in mind that not even 10% of all start-ups make it to an exit, only going up to 1/3 if they are at least seed-funded. This is not to scare you away but needs to be mentioned as part of a reality check! Nevertheless, my advice to you is that if you feel positive about the company, the team, and that you believe you have found your niche to add value, do follow your gut feeling. Being at the right place at the right time, feeling the zeitgeist, is not something tangible – if you feel the energy and have conducted your homework, give it your all, because the truth is also: the higher the risk, the more you potentially can get out of it.

That is also why I have not listed any **monetary** aspects until now. I simply do not believe that salary will be a useful scalability or cultural-fit indicator. At least it wasn't for me, when I was on the verge of deciding whether I believed in the potential of the business to succeed and its fit for me personally. When Jean-Daniel and I discussed me potentially joining his company, Captain Train, as COO, you might find it interesting to learn that we didn't speak about money at all for a long time and even when we did, it was an exchange of just a couple of emails. It just wasn't that important to me. You might think, what a snobby remark and easy to say, when you already have a lot of money. But I hadn't. I come from a modest background and had only started working 7 years previously, living in one of the most expensive cities in the world. Yet, money just wasn't critical in my decision to join. Instead, I had taken my decision quickly, based on our shared vision for the project, which was to make the most sustainable mode of transport more accessible, and our shared values for people and culture. Also, I had obviously conducted the detailed reality check described above. Then I was keen to meet the other co-founders to understand from them why they wanted out, before I spoke to the partners and the board of Captain Train. They confirmed my feeling that I wanted to work with them on this project. I now knew that I could trust them to be honest with me at every step along our joint adventure. And as a result, I took a big risk and resigned with 6-months' notice from a major CEO position in a safe corporate haven before we had even raised the money to go the next step. I knew, when we shook hands, that we shared profound and similar values. It meant that we were going to make this happen, and I am so glad I did so, as the spirit in which it was started sustained the whole way through the adventure.

However, I'm not saying don't negotiate your package. You definitely should at this stage and prior to signing anything. For me, shares, more than salary, were an important driver, like a carrot before my eyes that helped me to make it through when times got tough. Consequently, and appreciating that this is an interesting topic which is rarely discussed in the open, allow me to make a short deviation on this matter.

The starting assumption is that when you work in a scaling business, you want to be there for the ultimate goal of a successful exit and for the passion to achieve that, not for security or stability. However, it is wrong to think that negotiating your package is seen as something negative. On the contrary, you might be expected to, as it gives an indication of your commercial and negotiation skills, which you might be hired for in the first place. But also, the other way round, the way this discussion will be conducted provides a first insight on the values, clarity and transparency on their side. Another misperception is around scale-ups not paying fairly. Obviously, when they are tiny, they don't have the same financial power as a huge corporate, but you might be pleasantly surprised how creative scale-ups become to appropriately remunerate specialists and other people they desperately need.

My key advice is that the exit perspective should determine your package negotiation. Don't put most of your effort into negotiating your monthly salary, but instead, look at what you potentially could make by staying with the project until its exit. If you do, you can be sure that you're aligned with the company's interest, which will make it easier to achieve your personal goals. I have had many examples where people negotiated their monthly salary up by, say, €300 net and in return accepted smaller variable and share parts. They then lost out on several €100k at the exit, and that hurts. Of course, the cities where most scale-ups are based are expensive, and I don't say don't care about your salary, but don't lose your focus on the endgame. You need to believe in the ultimate success point, and if the above reality check was positive, you should fully get on board. Otherwise, there is no point of joining or trying to scale this enterprise in the first place. If you do however and you negotiate your package in this light, with scaling and exiting being integral to your plan, then your personal balance sheet at the end will show a multiple of what you would have made even in top management in a big corporate across the same time span.

To illustrate the components of the negotiating strategy of your remuneration package (and future increases during the journey), I have developed what I call the retro-exit-pyramid in scale-ups. It's a top-down approach where you start with your goal, the exit, and negotiate backwards.

A monetary package usually consists of 3 components:

1. Gross annual fixed salary
2. Variable yearly bonus, linked to your personal and company objectives
3. Shares linked to the exit

And for top specialists or C-level people who need extra convincing to join, in rare cases, there can even be awarded a welcome bonus.

My pyramid strongly suggests that it is important to spend most energy on negotiating from the exit downward, to gain the biggest influence on achieving the optimum total remuneration package. This implies however that your salary is the least important component, which might be against your sense of security and what you would usually do. But again, you are in this position because you believe it will work out and you are keen to participate in a potential exit as fully as possible.

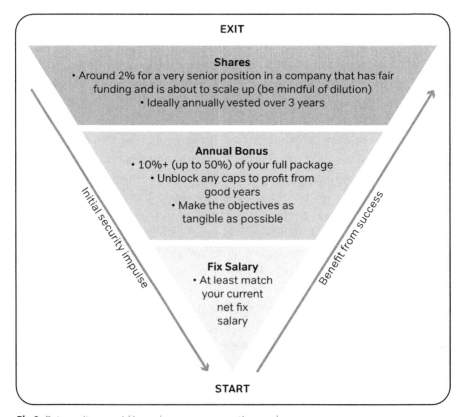

Fig 2: *Retro-exit-pyramid in scale-ups: remuneration package*

If you negotiate on this basis and come to an agreement, it's a classic win-win-situation: the company knows that you're invested for the whole journey and you have a strong incentive to make it a huge success. A good cross-check is to come to work and not feel like you are working for someone or for a company, but rather feel that you are working on your own project. And once you have decided to join and start to scale-up, you should forget about any of what has been discussed in this chapter and focus on getting the scaling phase right and enjoy the ride, to put yourself in the best possible position to succeed.

So, let's get to it.

TOP 3
Takeaways

1. Does the business have a clear set of values and goals, and do you share them?

2. Does the company have a solid foundation to grow on?

3. Is there a (hidden) roof that could hinder a successful scaling process?

CHAPTER 2

The Early Scaler Catches the Exit

Y ou have now taken the decision to scale up a business. This could be your own business or the one you feel is worth joining and investing in as if it were your own. This chapter is about the beginning of the scaling phase, which is likely to become one of the most intense of your professional life. We will look at each area of the business separately in greater detail during the course of this book. To start with, there are various crucial things that should be looked at as early as possible, as they touch on the company as a whole as well as on you personally and can't wait a day longer to be made right. This chapter talks about these fundamental elements that will make your scale-up ride smoother, ensuring that fewer corrections are needed and increasing the likelihood of success.

Before we go in medias res though, it is worth laying out some academic groundwork on what the subject of this book, the scale-up, is, and what I mean when I speak about growing and scaling. The OECD defines a scale-up as a company which grows at least 20% over three years, with 10 or more employees at the start of that period. In a nutshell, it's a next level start-up. A scale-up combines two capabilities: it can scale, and it can grow. While these two terms are often misused interchangeably, you need both to achieve your goal.

Scaling has made it into the top ranks of any professional buzzword list and is used all too often incorrectly as a synonym for growth. Among the multiple differences between the two, there is one that you should specifically remember: **growth** is linear – you add resources to your enterprise (people, tech, etc.) and you get an output that will be proportional to your input. In other words, your revenue increases at the same pace as you invest. You could grow faster by making a shortcut and acquire another company. I will however park that option until the final part of this book and focus instead on adding new geographies (new markets) or new verticals (new customer groups).

Scaling has this crucial difference – you add revenue at a greater rate than the investment made. From your microeconomic lectures, you might remember the concept of economies of scale, which drives at decreasing the cost of every additional unit of output. Let's make that more tangible with an example from the digital world. You operate an online platform that has 300 customers on it. To maintain this platform, you will need 3 people. Ergo, you need 1 person per 100 customers. If your build out your platform to serve 5 times more customers (1500), but only need 2 additional people to host it, your ratio goes down to 1 person for 300 customers and with that your cost per customer. At this point, you might think, that's awesome, give me the magic recipe! And I would answer, it isn't magic, it's rather just a matter of adding fundamental structure and processes to your company to make this happen.

Reading the above hopefully gives you an indication on why I am being so insistent on making it a priority to build out the scaling foundation as early as possible. Perhaps, adding a visual to your mind can make it even clearer: I always try to picture it as a jigsaw puzzle. You try to put together your 1000-piece puzzle, but most of the pieces are showing the sea and clouds, with 50 shades of blue, so what do you do first? You don't start putting together one wave in the middle, just because you have found two linking pieces by accident. No, you would get completely lost later on. Instead, you start by finding the pieces that have edges and try to put them together to build out the frame first. On this basis you then grow and scale the rest on and within it. This is exactly what we're trying to do in this chapter – spending a bit more time in the beginning to build out the frame first, to ensure that we can move faster later. What might seem like a detour is in fact a shortcut.

The challenge to all that is the beauty of us being human. What I mean is that we function in routines and habits that are complicated to change. So, I do appreciate that your initial instinct is to move forward fast, fixing quick patches. This pattern is hard to unlearn, but not impossible, when you begin to shape your mind in the right direction. That's why this chapter is about setting up the business itself, while the next chapter is about the investment in you personally to be the scaling rock in this adventure.

Let's start with what should be done on **the business side** today, to make your life easier tomorrow. Here is my **top-10-list of the things you should consider now to be able to scale successfully**. They are not to be read as a chronological list, as they can be carried out simultaneously. You might find some of the following obvious at first glance, but would you have implemented them at this stage?

1. **Create unique and optimised content**

   We live in a world where a crucial part of our success depends on the way search engines rank us, and this is based on our content history: the quality and the continuity of editing. The other option, to buy our way to growth, is, unfortunately, not an endlessly scalable model. Therefore, your task is clear: add the greatest possible quantity of content and ideally start yesterday so that search engines have time to digest it and include the correct keywords from the outset. Write unique and relevant content, and create backlinks so that people will spend more time on your site. A rule of thumb is that it can easily take a year for you to secure a good ranking, also depending on what your competition does. Think big and anticipate from the start, using Google Analytics to identify a list of the top 15 countries and languages that your clients come from today. Then have your top pages translated into as many languages as possible, and have natives proofread your content before publishing. The marginal cost for adding an extra language is lower than you think if you implement this from the outset. The impact on winning new customers and increasing your sales numbers can be huge, not to mention the great story you will be able to tell the press and your investors.

2. **Create a scalable brand**

   There are various factors to take into account here. The most important one is that you want to avoid needing to change your domain name. Picture it like in the board game *Monopoly*, as when you do this you go all the way back to *Go*, but you don't collect any money from the banker! All your great content impact in the previous point starts from zero again. As a domain change is often a consequence of a **change in branding**, it is so important to get your branding right early on. I say this from experience, having gone through three rebrandings in one year: from 'Capitaine Train' to 'Captain Train', then to 'Captain Train, a Trainline Company' and finally to 'Trainline' across the whole group. Let me tell you, even handled in the best possible way, using the greatest branding experts, this was an utter pain in the ass. On top of the ranking issue, it is expensive, it takes focus from what's really important, and it creates frustration for teams who have an attachment towards your brand. While you can change colours and images without too many drastic side effects, your brand name and its spelling really should be decided on from the outset through the rest of the journey.

   So, to create a scalable brand today, consider the following:

   i.   Does your brand work in all languages (pronunciation) and design/identity (colours and symbols can have different meanings and associations, especially in Asia) in all markets that you might potentially be working in? When I worked with Deutsche Bahn, their logo read "Die Bahn". Try pronouncing "Die" in English…

ii. Does your brand name have enough maturity, or could it be interpreted as cute when you're little but stand in the way when you're growing older? Like a baby that is named Peppy who hates her parents for this by the time she turns 18 and just wishes for another name. Our Captain brand was falsely being linked to pirates sometimes, which made it increasingly more complicated to explain that we were legitimate partners and not illegally hacking data. Discuss your branding with your customers as much as you can, to be sure that you consider all important elements, as it can often take outsiders to spot some glaring problems. Then test before you decide. Observing reactions from a focus group can then be a good final check.

iii. Think ahead and secure licences for domains in every country where you intend to trade, now and in the future. You do not want this to be an impediment to growth in the future, particularly as the price to buy back a brand can be huge if, down the line, you are committed to using that brand in other territories.

3. Build a flexible tech infrastructure

The following thought will be unpopular among some of the tech gurus out there who have shaped the start-up world with their creative individualism. Nevertheless, my strong advice is that you need to accommodate large and flexible tech capacity increases from the start. We have all hosted our servers inhouse in the beginning, trying to create our very own infrastructure or have maybe used a niche software or hip programming language as a principle to make a difference. But no matter what you think today, this approach is not scalable.

The day will come when you need to outsource and move to the cloud, using larger teams, and move away from individual solutions to something that is compatible with the mainstream. Finding 50 engineers all at once is a challenge you may well face, as we did, when scaling up rapidly. Trying to find so many with a niche programming language is an unnecessary complication you do not want to give yourself. And with that in mind, do yourselves a favour and avoid at all costs what I have seen not working in the beginning of my own scale-up experience. Here is my one and only worst-3 hitlist, which would haunt every investor's worst nightmare.

i. We missed out on 80% of potential new customers because our server crashed due to extremely high traffic immediately after an unbelievably expensive TV commercial aired.

ii. Our external platform service provider's premises burned down and because they didn't have any back-up, our website was down for a whole day.

iii. When our one key IT specialist decided to leave (not on great terms), I didn't sleep well as we had no back-up and had created an unsustainable dependency on him.

4. Test your product

My biggest learning in relation to the product is to ship fast and test your way to perfection. Put first versions live in production to see how they go and then test, test, test from the beginning to learn from this. And, to not exclude any customers, I discourage you from implementing a process of registration for people to gain access to your service. Be inclusive from the start and don't force people to create an account, unless this is embedded in your business model. Imposing a closed, secret club makes everything more difficult, and becomes harder to change every day you grow.

Put in place the right test environment so that you can grow and scale from your own learnings. Task all your teams to speak to your customers on a regular basis to make sure this stays at the heart of everyone's attention. Think of quick and effective ways to reach a representative cross-section of your likely customer base. At Captain Train, we sent our teams to Starbucks to have them interview random people, who proved to be remarkably representative of our target audience. We asked them to test our product in exchange for a free chocolate chip almond chai latte with caramel mint flavouring, or whatever that week's special was... Now, what was interesting was that our teams regularly came back depressed, because what the teams loved turned out not to be necessarily what the potential customers needed. So, this proved to be invaluable market research, conducted quickly and cheaply! And the key lesson learned was that we must never develop a product for ourselves, but always only for our precious customers. This important lesson is always scalable!

5. Grow your customer service centre flexibly

Adopting a human-based customised approach to customer service, ensuring that you answer each customer individually, may be one of your top USPs and marketing tools in the beginning in your home market, but unfortunately it is just not endlessly scalable.

When you start adding new markets that perhaps require new languages to serve in and on a 24/7 basis due to time differences, or new target groups with specific needs, you will need to add more automated layers of service. Try also to allow for flexibility to anticipate the next strike wave, natural disaster or terrorist attack that will hit and may leave your teams swamped with support tickets. Another scale-up barrier is that recruiting to the same level of quality inhouse is too slow and costly at a certain level, and so I suggest looking into an outsourced flexible second level of customer support as an add-on, without jeopardising your core quality level.

6. Plan your finances

You need to find a way to finance your growth and to set the basis for scaling. To do so, you need a clear, detailed and comprehensive business case (BC). If you are not clear, investors are unlikely to be convinced, and you then need to spend a disproportionate amount of time and energy in finding the necessary sources of investment. If that all goes wrong, it could mean the end of the adventure before it has even started.

What does a clear BC look like? Ideally, it outlines three investment scenarios: a bullish, over-positive one, a 'worst case', and then a realistic one that you are fully convinced you can deliver against. All plans must anticipate a realistic burn rate and necessary fundraising, along with detailed delivery and KPI milestones. You then need to ensure that you start your next fundraising series early enough, as this always takes longer than expected, and I'm not even talking about the possible effects of another Covid-19 scenario. This planning should then be internalized into your business case, which you also use as a basis for your presentation in which you outline your way to move to an exit. Investors always want to see a graph that goes exponentially up to the right – you need to demonstrate that you have located your scaling mechanisms and ideally have already proved them working in parts, so that €1 invested becomes significantly more in return.

7. Build your organisation by creating clear decision-making structures

What might sound boring and like corporate bullshit is in fact the most underrated element to impactful scaling in my view. Being crisp on how you come to decisions and being clear on who is in charge of each project is essential to making the organisation work effectively while you scale and grow heavily. When the largest table has become too small to gather the whole team around it over lunch, the flow of information and decisions will change. Judging from the past decade of my professional experience, dealing with changes to the size of the team represents, I would estimate, 75% of all structural issues to scaling. And that is the main reason I moved from the corporate to the start-up world, because I felt that I could add value by driving the necessary change but knowing that it is much more fun implementing it in a smaller setting with mostly superstars. What it came down to in the end was implementing the following 3 things:

i.   **Draw up an organisational chart** and think about what it should look like in 9 months' time and in 3 years from now, and how you can structure it today to allow for exponential growth.

ii. **Have detailed job descriptions** for the people working with you today as well as for the key roles you are looking for in the near future. Then apply a great tool called RACI: **Responsible, Accountable, Consulted** and **Informed**. Who needs to be consulted before taking a decision, who is the approver and will be held accountable for it and who needs to be informed after? And most importantly, who is the one person responsible for the topic in question? Be careful to not end up with several people in the R role, with many cooks spoiling the broth. If you get this way of thinking right on a small level at the outset, people will internalise it and this will add to the structure needed to make the organisation scalable. This tool has the power to change the whole team dynamic for the better, by empowering and trusting in experts, avoiding overlapping, achieving faster delivery and more qualitative output to increase your team's motivation significantly.

iii. **Clarify the roles of the founder(s)** and avoid one of the common reasons why start-ups fail – having the founder onboard for the exit may increase your valuation, but don't keep them onboard at any price. Be clear on how operationally involved the founder(s) want to remain over time and agree on relevant milestones. One way to do this is to keep the founder in a more external-facing president or chairman role, with a COO being the internal general manager in charge of managing the company. One of the reasons why Captain Train was so successful was because two of the co-founders, having created a great product, then stepped back from the business before the scaling phase took off, as they decided for themselves that they were not the right cast for what was needed from there. Having the ability to see that deserves a lot of respect I find.

And what about culture you might ask – now, isn't that the single most important thing? Well, yes, absolutely, but aren't the implementation of these three things above at an early stage a strong message of how serious you are about culture? They will create more impact than any pretty chart explaining your intentions and values. Start by being a role model – say thank you, show appreciation and empathy, take and give feedback and try to be as transparent as possible. All this is a good starting point to a topic that will play an important part in the people chapters later on.

8. Transfer know-how

Implementing a knowledge store will not only make you sleep better but will make an auditor's eyes shine during any due diligence and consequently help to increase your valuation. Brain drain is the common term for people leaving with all their expertise and leaving you with nothing, making it difficult for new joiners to have a smooth onboarding. Therefore, setting up an internal wiki knowledge base, linking sources and explaining the company's functioning should not be postponed a day longer.

And you can even use the input for parts of your own playbook. To share my personal philosophy on this subject: I tried to operate my businesses in a manner to be replaceable, to never make it about me as a person, but about the role that I represented for the company. Ideally, if I got run over by a bus tomorrow, everything could be picked up easily. It sounds cold, but you owe this to the business you have helped to create, and you should be so humble as to put the wellbeing and continued success of the business first.

Furthermore, regardless of whether you are based in an English-speaking country or elsewhere, use this moment to switch into English entirely for all official conversation and documentation. You may well have non-English speakers joining your organisation at some point, and it will make their start with you a whole lot more productive from day one.

9. Find the right office

Despite working remotely becoming more common, a trend of course greatly accelerated by the 2020/21 global pandemic, your office should be set up as your central get-together space to exchange views and ideas. More than this, it should be an important escape from home to help you to focus on work and interact with your colleagues and feel and share their energy. To create stability, it is important to not move offices too often, as that can be time- and energy-consuming and creates unnecessary friction without adding much value. There will be so much change during the years while your company and teams scale that all of you involved need a steady rock when there are rough seas ahead. Of course, I understand that you wouldn't want to spend an extra €10k now on office space that you might not fully occupy until later. However, keep in mind that finding the right offices can take many months in major start-up hot spot locations, and you don't want to end up squeezing people into tiny spaces and, even worse, having to damage morale by, for example, banning table soccer like we had to at one point! What you need is a flexible platform on which to grow – so, try to anticipate that as early as possible and avoid moving.

Explore creative solutions like finding spaces that you can rent out in parts first, but with the option to take over an additional floor at a later point, or rent the whole building and sublet it until you need it yourself. Also, start thinking about the look of your offices. Are they going to be prestigious enough for receiving your (future) customers or partners and, most importantly as part of your employer brand, will they attract new colleagues into a landscape where you are competing for the best talent? The final point to take into consideration is the location of the office. Ideally, from the beginning, choose an area where there are several start-ups. You will find that there is a different vibe: it's young, vibrant and up-and-coming, attracting fashionable restaurants and bars. Take a tour of the area and check out the types of shops and apartment buildings in the neighbourhood. All these are indicators of how attractive the area will be to the type of team members you will be looking for. If you need to move, it might be easier to move next door instead of to the other side of the city, where you risk losing people who can't commute easily to your offices anymore. However, it will be worth the extra investment and initial disruption, and you might be surprised how many people choose or leave companies because of the choice and location of their offices. On top of this, potential investors can be impressed by amazing offices which help to make manifest your ambitions, without making it a financial risk.

10. Create ambassadors

Talk about your project wherever you can, and don't worry that somebody could copy you – if it was that easy, it wouldn't be the right one to work on in the first place. The objective is to create some hype and receive valuable feedback from the outside world in return. Identify potential partners and create an exclusive club with them. When you involve them early, and you provide them with privileged information to underline how special they are to you, they can become strong allies and they can serve you as multiplicators for your cause. The scaling effect of this for you can be huge, as it can open doors and help to create an image of successful intriguing mystery. Think big! We were lucky in that we found a way for the most successful tech business in the world, Apple, to take notice of us and choose to get involved with us in this way, and they helped Captain Train at an early stage to be able to speak at the European Commission. Use incubators who can put you in contact with the big players and some selective members of the press who can publish exclusive information upfront. It becomes a win-win situation when you succeed: those who have promoted you in this way at this previewing stage are seen as being perceptive early adopters and, in return, you have gained some excellent free-of-charge ambassadors for your brand.

Top 10 things to prepare today for scaling-up your business

1.	Create as much *content* as early as possible
2.	Decide on your *brand and stick to it*
3.	Avoid niche-dependent *IT solutions* to be able to scale
4.	Put your *product* live quickly and *test, test, test*!
5.	Set up your *customer service* for flexible growth
6.	Have a clear *business case and funding plan, including* how to get to an exit
7.	Write an *org-chart*; apply the RACI; include the founders
8.	Set up *an internal knowledge base* in English
9.	Grow in the same *office* (building) or neighbourhood
10.	Find yourself *strong allies*

TOP 3
Takeaways

1. Create as much content as early as possible

2. Decide on your brand and stick to it

3. To be able to scale, avoid niche-dependent IT solutions

CHAPTER 3

Becoming a Corporate Athlete

M ost people say that living through a scale-up to an exit is a sprint, not a marathon. I disagree, for me it was in fact both – you are running as fast as you would for a 100-metre sprint, while needing to sustain that pace over a distance of at least a hundred kilometres, every day for several years. I don't know about your level of fitness, but I wouldn't have survived that if I hadn't learned some techniques to look after myself to get through the whole scaling phase in some sort of sustainable manner. And it's never too late to start.

I am conscious that it's never easy to take time out of your busy schedule to take a step back while you're trying to move fast. But you will come to see that stepping back to move forward faster is not in fact a contradiction – they rather go hand in hand. Try to picture a plane which you are trying to fill up with kerosine. And while you're concentrating on adding kerosine to take off fast and go as far as you can, you don't even realise that the tail rudder is yet to be attached, which you won't see, standing under the wings. Zooming out on a regular basis to look at your plane from the distance to see where you stand on progress will help you to evaluate what the most urgent issues are to solve first before taking off, instead of adding the 100th tonne of fuel to a non-operating plane. This goes equally for your business and for you **as a person**. You only have limited personal resources, which you will need to take care of even more when you have entered the scale-up phase.

Fig 3: *Cavemen with square wheels – unknown source*

You need to think about what you can do to recharge your batteries and focus on what's most important to you so that you use your energy most efficiently. Just like on the business side, it's important to start developing the right reflexes at the beginning, as it gets harder to unlearn bad habits during the course of a bumpy ride. Investing in yourself sounds like the most obvious thing in the world, but unfortunately still has connotations of weakness or failure to it and is therefore hardly ever discussed. I believe, to the contrary, it should be considered as at least as important as the pure business side. After all, your body and your mind are your most crucial resources for your success and consequently for that of the business. If you embrace this fact and adapt your life accordingly, it will become a superpower which will get you there all the way. That said, the following is a combination of my personal learnings and what I have taken from hundreds of hours of coaching on both the giving and the receiving end. Take a step back with me to read the following and prepare for the ride that is most likely to be the most exhausting one you have ever embarked on.

We all have phones, and we all anxiously follow the battery level displayed at the loading bar continuously, trying to save energy as much as we can when it gets too low, and then recharge it as soon as we get to a power plugin. This is precisely what you should be doing with **your personal energy level as well**. The fuller and greener your bar is, the more energy you can expend. But when you feel you're getting lower to the yellowish part of the bar you need to find out what your own equivalent is to closing the 25 apps running in the background and plugging in your charging cable. Otherwise, you will feel empty before you know it. However, as we are all human beings with individual needs, there is no passe-partout solution, and you will need to find out what model works best for you personally.

Just as when you are formulating a successful business service, the best way is to test and learn, in this case choosing from the next pages what works best for you.

In *The Making of the Corporate Athlete*, which you ought to become if you want to make it to an exit it one piece, Loehr & Schwartz suggest that there are four levels of energy, which I have regrouped into three categories:

Spiritual	The purpose you joined for	Should be clear after Chapter 1
Physical	Your fitness and balance	**Recharging your batteries**
Emotional	Your feelings when stressed	**Spending your energy most efficiently**
Mental	Mind space – time to think	

Recharging your batteries

Let's start with the basics: a **healthy work-life balance** to charge your batteries to the maximum, every single day. It will help you to increase your productivity, make better decisions, be less stressed, be fairer in your judgments and more resilient. What works for me as a foundation to get there is:

- 7.5 hours of **sleep** – the earlier I go to bed before midnight the more effective that is for me.
- Enjoying at least one **warm healthy meal** a day – cooking it myself relaxes me most.
- 2 weekly sessions of **physical activity** of 30 minutes each – tennis and swimming work for me.

But that's just the foundation. I also gain positive energy through people and things I care deeply about: **spending time with my best friends and close family**, especially my baby boy, as well as ecstatically listening to music, are part of my magic juice to disconnect and to put things into perspective. That can even imply that having a great night out might make me more productive the next day, even when I have only slept for 5 hours. And I'm explicitly *not* talking about energy kicks like legal or illegal substances. Those, just like chocolate (OK, I'm totally addicted to that unfortunately) might give you short time energy back, but they might break your battery and then make it impossible to recharge until it's fixed again. What I have found to work if you need a quick refill, especially in the afternoon hours when your natural efficiency curve goes down, is drinking a lot of **water, eating fruit** and, if you get a chance, take a **power nap**: 3 minutes give me back an hour. By the way, the power nap is a topic that in Japan is not taboo at all but even encouraged by some companies – 20-minute naps are proven to have great effects on productivity.

On top, you need **regular breaks** to fully reset your mind. Start with the weekends. Some people work through the entire weekend as if it wasn't there, in order to get all their work done. Or they start work on Sunday night at the expense of not sleeping well and then getting a sleepy start into the new week. My magic recipe is something in-between. I have successfully forced myself over the past decade to take one day off entirely each week. I don't look at my phone, I refrain from managing any personal administration either and focus on just being in the moment. Grab fresh bread in the morning, look at the sky and just live the day with your loved ones. This state of mind prolonged to 14 days (ideally 21) is what I call a holiday. My trick has been to let one person know how to reach me, in case the house is on fire, but I will not proactively look at my emails or read any messages. And let me tell you, the house has never burned down, and I have received only one text and two calls in all these years. Every time, I have come back fully recharged and ready to rumble.

Can you say precisely where you get your energy from? If not, this is the time to figure that out. Look at yourself from a meta level for a couple of weeks and try to understand how you function. Test yourself on what works and what doesn't work for you, and what it is you need to fill up your tanks on a regular basis. And the process to get there is time well invested, because you will become many times more productive and will gain time back in return. In the end, I'm sure, we agree: It's not about how much you work, it's about how productive you are. This brings us to the next part of this chapter: **using your time and energy in the most efficient way, focusing on what's most impactful**.

Spending your energy most efficiently

Recharging your batteries is fundamental, but not worth much if you are not spending your freshly gained energy wisely. However, we aren't robots, and we are influenced by everything that happens around us. Therefore, accepting that there will be less productive days is part of managing expectations for yourself. Sometimes, you waste less energy when you call it a day early, recharge and then come back more productive the next day. However, it is critical that you understand the difference between a bad day and an ongoing downward trend that you would want to break quickly, as here illustrated in this diagram.

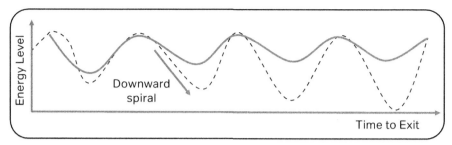

Fig 4: *Energy-Level to Exit Diagram*

The closer you get to the bottom of the dotted line, the harder it is to climb back out of your hole again. At a certain point, it becomes a true downward spiral that eats up all your energy and then makes it hard to recharge your batteries again. Therefore, before you even get into that vicious circle, you need your alarm bells to go off and your reflexes and habits to kick in, automatically initiating a mechanism that helps you to fight against it and move up again. The goal is to keep the extremes of the amplitudes relatively close together, with the lows as high as possible, ideally staying at the levels of the solid line. This all sounds great in theory, so let me suggest the following three tools that hopefully can serve to create your reality:

1. Separate content from form
2. Take time to think
3. Evaluate your time management

All three tools start with the same presumption, that **we have a tendency to dive right in when it gets hectic**. We become reactive, operational trouble shooters and tend to get lost in the details, trying to quicker-fix any problems. But in this manner, we hardly ever sustainably solve the issue at its roots. At best, we find a quick patch, but usually we make it worse in the long-run and the situation might even backfire, which can really hurt you in the middle of the scaling phase. I have seen burnouts, and small workarounds exploding, derailing whole exits at the last minute. Make sure this doesn't happen and **take a step back first** before you dive in, to make sure you see clearly the source and identify the solution to the problem to make it disappear sustainably once and for all.

1. Separate content from form

This first exercise is probably the one I have used most often. We all know the following situation: a discussion gets heated, you get an email with an issue that annoys you, and you feel like you want to react instantly. My piece of advice is simple: don't! Everything that is a reaction to something that makes you feel negative will not help to solve the issue but will consume your positive energy. Don't get me wrong, I'm not saying avoid conflicts or hold back with what needs to be said or decided. An argument can even create value and more energy, but not when you get emotional on a personal level. Instead, question yourself on your overall objective and how this issue ranks in this context. It will help you to put the issue in perspective and make the right call, and eventually save you both time and energy. Once you have cleared your head, everything will look smaller and less significant when you look at it from more of a distance.

Before I had started embracing this practice, I spent a lot of time apologizing and repairing the glass that I broke in these kinds of situations by creating a disproportionate fuss. No matter what happens, **stay calm and don't react impulsively**, especially not in meetings with more than one other person in the room. Instead, exit the situation by ending it calmly, explaining that there won't be an immediate solution or decision at this point, and then take a deep breath. I have sometimes cancelled my next meeting and taken a walk. Fresh air helps, or I have called a friend or listened to music, things that have made my mind shift to positivity again. The next thing to do is to separate the content of the issue from the form. Were you annoyed with **what** was said or **how** it was said? This is an important difference to figure out, as it is the indicator of what really needs to be addressed. I remember receiving an email that had a tone to it that made me want to throw my computer out of the window, but in fact the content was exactly what I needed. Until I stopped responding straightaway, I would have let the form cloud my view of the content, and I would have written back immediately that the tone was unacceptable without even realising that I had received confirmation on what I needed to achieve my goal. Now, I still sometimes write the answer to structure my thoughts and help me to calm down, but I don't send it straightaway. Instead, I ask myself what messages I want to send and balance out whether it's worth making a general comment on the tone for the sake of culture or not. Fresh, professional and goal-oriented thinking has been restored, with a clear mind back in charge.

And, either way, emails are never a good way to solve an issue. Instead, pick up the phone or see the person with doors closed, and let them know what they could do better next time. Be a role model and **encourage positive behaviour**, starting with yourself. And 20 minutes later the issue is sustainably solved before it has even had the chance to become a problem to the wider teams. And not only have you made an important contribution to the company culture, but you have also set a focus on what really counts, spending your energy wisely.

2. Take time to think

Now, to be able to base your judgment on your priorities, you need to become aware of them first. In a busy and reactive work environment, this is easier said than done. There is hardly ever time to think things through. Others will almost never let you finish your thoughts, and when you are finally alone and not swamped by emails, you most likely start to tackle everything else that you have on your desk. For this purpose, based on one of my favourite author's book, Nancy Kline's *Time to Think*, I have developed something for myself that is easy as pie. I call it the **blank paper exercise**.

Ever since I started adding this to my schedule, it has become the most valuable asset of my week. It has helped me to understand what it is that I need and want to work on, and I would not have made it to any exit in one piece without it. Here is how it goes: every week, you block one hour in your agenda, ideally always at the same time – Friday afternoon has worked well for me because it has helped me to clear my head before the weekend and get my mind around what I need to focus on from Monday morning.

Now, the challenge with these things is to not compromise this slot with all the other things you didn't find time for in the week. Therefore, be clear on what needs to happen and that you do use this designated hour for the exercise. For me, it was mostly about the place: I usually did it while traveling, when I was without a connection and saw the world pass by from my train or plane window. If I was in the office, I left my desk, my phone and my laptop and locked myself in another room, just taking a blank sheet of paper and a pencil with me.

You have now changed your setting and created a good **thinking environment** for you to gain the necessary altitude to start the exercise that literally only has one question: "What are the most important topics at the moment you should be working on". Jot down whatever comes to mind first. Then, you might want to stack-rank what you have jotted down and add more details on the steps to achieve them. Over time, you will develop a routine and become much clearer with yourself on your priorities. Becoming a pro, you might be ending up only needing this every other week and just for 30 minutes. What counts is that you allow time to think for yourself. Coming out of one of these sessions, I still feel amazing and energetic every time. However, coming back to reality holds a challenge for you, which is the realisation that what you should be working on is not necessarily what you *are* working on. But this shouldn't discourage you – quite the opposite, you can now use your newly gained clarity. Visualise the output you want to achieve by repeating verbal statements to yourself until you see a noticeable behavioural change in you. It sounds esoteric, but it's a powerful tool, the impact of which can even be measured in your brain waves and is often referred to as **autosuggestion**. Once you have understood that the desired changes start with yourself, your clarity and your mindset, you are perfectly equipped to close the gap between what you should be working on and what you find yourself working on and will stop letting others dictate your agenda.

3. Evaluate your time management

Let's now use a final exercise to understand what it is that you're actually working on – it's called the **Time-Management-Pie-Chart-Exercise**. For at least two weeks, you take note of everything you do and enter it into predefined categories. I suggest a two-dimensional approach: look at what you spend your time doing (reading emails, sitting in meetings etc.) and look at your objectives and other topics you work on.

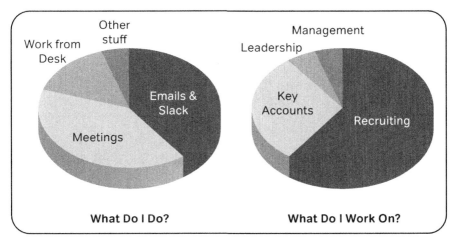

Fig 5: *Time-Management-Pie-Chart-Exercise*

Sadly, the outcome is often that one does not spend most of the time working on one's objectives nor on thinking about how to achieve them. But the good news is, once you have identified the difference between what you should work on and what you do work on now, you can start closing the gap by asking yourself consistently: am I spending my time on what adds most value for me and the business, and if not, why am I still doing it?

I was once asked: "How many times a day do you empty your letter box at home?" And I said: "Once a day". "Then why do you look at your email inbox every 5 minutes?" It's a good question, and the answer is, it doesn't make any sense. Set rules for yourself – don't answer emails throughout the day but set slots for it.

By continuously going through loops like this one, you will more and more focus on working on what you consider to be your priorities. You will have more time on your hands to operate at the highest possible energy levels yet working more productively and adding more value than before. These are all essential prerequisites for the necessary personal and mental state needed to work successfully through the scale-up phase that starts right here, right now.

TOP 3
Takeaways

1. Be very mindful of your energy levels

2. Make time to think

3. Focus on your time management

SECTION II

The Scaling Phase

CHAPTER 4

People. People. People.

T he next four chapters will look in greater detail at how to scale each of the main areas of your business. In this and the following chapter, we focus on people, followed by product & tech, and conclude with marketing. There is a reason why I decided to begin with the people part and even split this into two chapters, one focusing on operational HR topics and the other on leadership. It is that, simply, I have never seen anything more impactful on the scaling process than getting your human resources right. The best project in the world is worth nothing if you don't bring in the right people, and then care about, develop and empower them to create the best possible culture to make a difference. You can buy their time with the salary you pay them, but neither their commitment nor their passion have a price tag. These need to be earned. Consequently, this chapter for me is a story of trust, integrity and understanding people as the complex human beings they are.

The importance of HR

If you haven't already done so, start by **hiring an HR person** tomorrow. When you are serious about wanting to scale, it can never be too early to do this, and the company can't be too small. If it's a budget question, start with a hybrid role, one willing to take over additional administrative tasks. And while you may well have your pay managed inhouse at the beginning, while you scale, you should successively outsource or automate more and more of your HR administrative processes, leaving your HR person to focus on the important aspects of the role. Why is this hire so crucial? For starters, like all important areas, it requires dedicated resources, extremely early in the game. Hiring an HR person also sends a clear statement to the teams that you are serious about the importance of looking after the people in your business.

From my own experience, managers in start- and scale-ups are often wrong about how they believe their teams are doing. So, you need to make sure that there is someone in place overseeing that 1:1s and reviews are happening in a thorough, regular, and consistent manner, so that these reveal the true nature of your team's morale, motivation and focus. With every day that the HR role is vacant, the risk increases of losing some of your superstars before you have even realised that there was a problem. I have seen this happen all too often, even despite red warning lights going off as big as fire trucks. There was simply no person or process in place to pick it up. An HR professional will help you to put in place the required evaluation and monitoring tools and should then be able to confront you with a healthy reality check on how your teams are performing and their level of commitment and motivation to the project.

Choosing the right person is key, as they will represent your values and therefore must live and breathe your culture. This will be your go-to-person with whom you are likely to share more with than anybody else over the next few years. Bring them on the journey with you and use this person as a sparring partner and not just as an executer. You need someone whom you can trust deeply, and who dares to tell you the truth. But their desk will also be the central contact point for your teams, the ideal channel for feedback and to take the temperature on many different topics, but somebody who is always rooting for you when it comes to it. I used my HR team all the time as a sounding board when introducing new ideas or delivering speeches, to understand how my messages were being received. I was absolutely blessed with the HR people I worked with and wouldn't have made it through to the end without their support and opinions. The ideal profile to look for at the early scaling phase is someone not too senior, yet with the potential to grow into a director role over time. Having a legal background can be an excellent bonus to round out the ideal profile.

Develop the right culture

Having an HR person on board is an excellent starting point, but it requires another key ingredient to put oil in the spokes. This is where we need to examine the company's **culture**. I find that this term is bandied about all too often but with all too little tangible, detailed definition. Just like a nation's, your company's culture will be unique to your shared values and to the attributes that will have developed as particular to your industry and country. The challenge is that this culture will need to evolve dramatically throughout your scale-up phase. Just as a nation would struggle to deal with tripling its size and economy in the space of a couple of years, so your business will need to cope with huge stresses and strains during its growth phase. The trick is to find the fine line between not being too static and yet not compromising your principal values while you grow.

Two aspects drive this cultural change during the scale-up phase – **the size of the team and the likely increase in external funding**. The greater the number of people in the business, the more difficult it becomes to guarantee an easy flow of information so that everyone can make informed decisions. As I mentioned earlier, this changes dramatically when your teams can no longer eat around the same table. This becomes even more problematic when even the entire kitchen becomes too small to seat everyone. When the team size reaches fifty people or more, you might need a second floor, and this gets even worse when you reach a hundred and you discover that there are Slack channels that you weren't even aware of. This becomes hard to accept for the people who have been with you from the beginning. This increased complexity demands skilled leadership to provide guidance and confidence. You need to ensure that there is clear internal communication, along with having an acceptance that experts will be making the right calls. Honestly, it's OK to not be involved in every decision anymore! The caveat is that this might begin to feel more like a company you work for rather than being your own project.

The second major influencer is the level of external investment. In the beginning, the company was steadily in the founder's hand and then progressively the team begins to hold parts of it. At some point, after a couple of fundraising rounds, as things move closer to the exit, in comes greater intervention and influence from a greater number of larger shareholders, complete with voting rights and a chair on your board. This now means that they can impact decisions, and remember, they are in it for one reason only, which is to earn back a multiple of the money they have invested. Therefore, they naturally only care about results, which can change dramatically the dynamic, the values and the culture of your business.

But what are these values? What, ideally, does a company culture consist of? The best way to illustrate the key elements is to adapt the *Dysfunctions of a Team* model by Patrick Lencioni. This is also the title of his book, which I strongly recommend that you read. I have used and adapted the categories and built-up layers defined in that model to create what I call the 'Culture Pyramid for Scale-ups'.

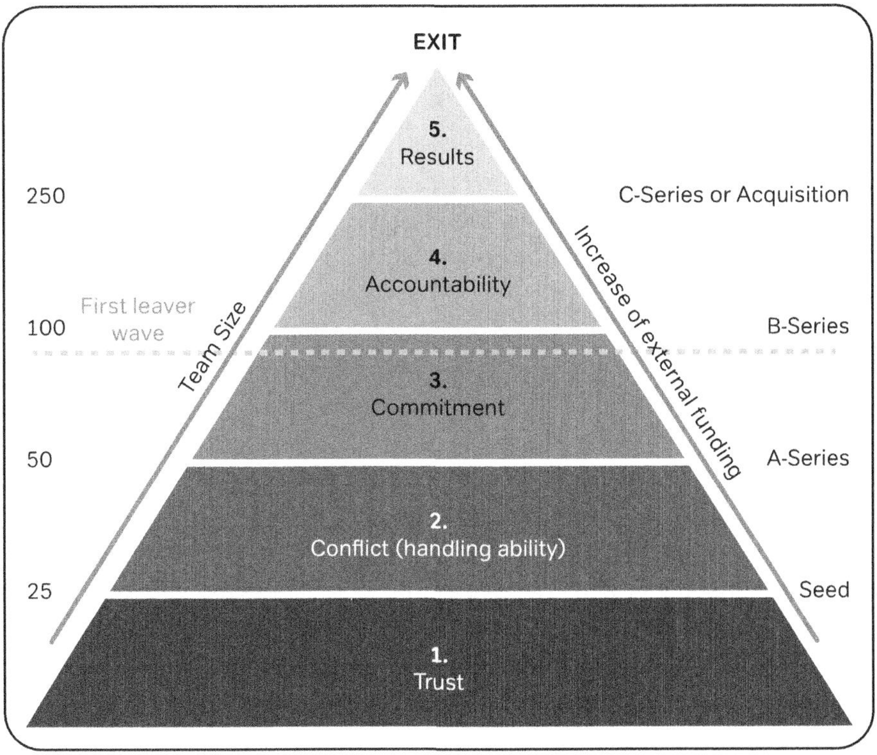

Fig 6: *Culture Pyramid for Scale-Ups*

1. **Trust:** You start by creating a foundation of trust. In the beginning, you are not making any money and new team-mates join because they are attracted by the project and the people. They are likely to be a group of idealists who care deeply about the idea of working together to disrupt and change the world. And as much as the tone of the culture in the beginning is set by the founder and then by the managers, with a growing team, every individual becomes an influencer in shaping your culture. But no matter what happens, the key element of trust, of feeling safe, of caring and showing mutual respect must remain untouchable and be the foundation to any other aspect of your culture which follows.

2. **Conflict:** As the teams and the complexity of topics increase, humans will disagree, and conflicts will occur. After perhaps some years of harmony, your first instinct might be to do everything you can to avoid these conflicts. That would be a shame, because embracing constructive feedback creates the opportunity for friction that can be creative, and a shining of light onto weak spots. It helps to create an environment that allows to make mistakes, disagree and cuts to the chase to solve problems and become better versions of ourselves. It takes time to

get used to this new addition to your culture, and it must always be carried out on the basis of trust and respect.

3. **Commitment:** In a world where you find that your teams are wearing your company branded t-shirts even at the weekend, it can seem impossible to imagine that commitment might become a challenge one day. But your business has now grown to such a size that you need to bring in some specialists from the industry that you trying to turn upside down. These new colleagues add a more corporate dimension to your culture, as they might not demonstrate the same passion for your project or are not bothered about having drinks with you after work. And that's OK, as long as they are doing a great job, the team as a whole remains committed, and they continue to act as your best external ambassadors. But be aware that this change will be tough on those employees who have been with you from the outset, and as a result a first wave of people leaving is, unfortunately, often unavoidable.

4. **Accountability:** A bigger team size requires a more detailed hierarchy to be put in place to make it more manageable. The problem then arises that people start thinking in silos and can end up caring more about their own areas of responsibility rather than about the wider company objectives. And when this happens, it can become challenging to hold people accountable. That is precisely why you need a tight organisation and a cohesive ethos which will bind together and empower those who are strong performers and are living your culture.

5. **Results:** Finally, the closer you move towards the exit, the more you will need to focus on output and results. That is fair enough and essential, because your teams are now large, and you have drawn in a significant amount of external funding. However, that focus on results is rarely the reason why somebody joined your project in the beginning. Remember, it was the human, individual aspect of it which they loved when they joined. Therefore, it is critical to break down results into motivational team objectives that everybody can relate to, and certainly ensure that, while you are focusing on results you don't forget about the four foundation layers of your cultural pyramid. However, if you have people who still believe that this is some sort of non-profit organisation, they need to leave the ship at this stage, or you won't likely make it to an exit.

I hope that it has become clearer why getting your culture right is hard but key. If you invest properly in it, you create an amazing spirit internally and a strong employer brand externally, which will make new recruits line up and investors dream. We quadrupled our teams to over 100 people in not even 9 months, to the point that I thought the postman was a new employee, and new joiners asked me what my role was when we bumped into each other in the kitchen. Whether that sounds awkward to you, or like me, just makes you laugh, just prepare for this to arrive fast. My next **top-10-list, of what you can do to help shape a great culture** in your company, can assist with that:

1. **Define the values of your company**

   It's a good thing to write them down, but it's worth nothing to just hang them on the wall if they don't match your actions.

2. **Make culture a topic**

   Talk about it when people join, to show that it's important to you and then remind your teams on a regular basis what you want the culture to be. In times of constant change, with many new joiners, I recommend making this speech at least twice a year.

3. **Start with yourself and be a role model**

   Make your words count and do what you say, without overpromising. Be transparent, readable and honest, giving others the opportunity to follow your thoughts and vision. Treat others like you want to be treated, with respect, saying thank you, really listening. Don't allow a bad day to jeopardise these values. And if there is a risk that day, stay at home!

4. **Be clear on the goal of the company**

   You know from the beginning that you are expecting to reach the top of the Culture Pyramid, and that you need people who want to join you on that mission and who also care about results. Of course, you still need to focus on meeting the needs of your customers, but be clear early on to everyone internally about your objective to exit. If you're not doing this, you risk a clash of culture, with the pain of well-established team members leaving later in the process, just when you need them most. However, see point 8 too!

5. **Prepare for change**

   All the above can be anticipated and accompanied by taking the time and trouble to explain change. And yet, you need to accept that change takes time. People need time to change, no matter how fast you want to move.

6. **Give and appreciate honest feedback**

   You are in this together, and you want to succeed as one team. You need to cut to the chase and know what is really going on. There is no room for blind spots, and nobody should be afraid of failing or of calling out an issue in a constructive manner.

7. Empower the right people

Culture will increasingly be passed on by the teams, and it is in your interest that those displaying the best cultural fit are given the most decision-making power. People should build a career through excellence, not just in delivery but also in using their emotional intelligence to treat people well and to live up to your culture.

8. Let go of poisonous people

One of the biggest mistakes I made was holding onto people for too long who didn't embrace the right culture anymore but had been those early employees with a great deal of expertise. The company needs to evolve to be successful. The culture will need to change with it and at that point is not necessarily suitable for all those people who were there at the beginning. In my example, the culture risked remaining being built around a few individuals as a way of keeping them onboard, making life unbearable for the rest of the team and seriously putting the success of the company at risk. Don't repeat this mistake, and ensure that you let people like that go asap. I understand that this may well be tough, particularly if you have had a long association with them, and they have been a key part of your early success. However, this is in fact best for them as much as it is for the company and the entire team.

9. Take responsibility for your community

Your culture should go beyond the people you work with and include your city and your environment. Helping others and supporting good causes as a group will also create a formidable team spirit.

10. Continue to trust your teams

This is particularly important as they grow. Great talent can work from anywhere – design a remote culture, allow for flexible working hours and let Generation Z appreciate their Yoga classes during lunchbreaks. The only thing you should worry about is that they achieve the business' objectives, leaving the how to them.

Other than that, there are a couple more elements that can have a huge impact on the culture that I would like to address separately here. They are still not sufficiently considered in today's business world, in my view: fair remuneration and diversity.

Fair remuneration

Remuneration is a crucial element to the perception of fairness within start- and scale-ups. It is not so much the absolute amount that is paid but rather what one earns relative to others. Captain Train was famous in the French start-up landscape for being entirely transparent on what everybody earned. There was a simple formula that allowed everyone to calculate their own and their colleagues' salaries and stock options. This included the following elements:

- What is your **department**? This could be customer service, marketing, tech, or product.
- How much **experience** do you have in your sector? Are you an expert in what you do?
- How much **seniority** do you have in the business? This was measured not in years, but on the level of impact on the company, and proved to be a far more robust way to reward loyalty.

On top of this, employees were given a ticket for urban transport, insurance and lunch vouchers. As any company matures, I suggest adding a fourth element to take into account when calibrating remuneration, and that is their **educational background**, to reward people's investment in their own human capital.

And all this paid off. This total transparency was greatly appreciated and was one of the reasons why people wanted to work with us in the first place. When I joined, this became a challenge, because I didn't fit into any of the categories and, because of confidentiality reasons, I couldn't go through the standard internal recruiting processes.

Then we hired country managers, a role that included several departments. And lastly, we brought in specialists and some more senior management for their expertise, and at this point the allegedly great tool became impossible to manage. Therefore, we needed to accept that **transparency has its limits**. So, my strong advice is to adjust the transparency tool when you hit a ceiling instead of pretending to be able to fit a square peg into a round hole. As, at that point you end up being the opposite of transparent. We hadn't provided sufficient explanation on that change, nor did we offer an alternative. As a result, our brilliant people came up with their own remuneration calculations which they published on the wiki. Unfortunately, they were no longer at all accurate, and this led to frustrations and a feeling of injustice. Learn from this mistake and communicate proactively, providing if necessary, a new tool that everyone can accept and understand.

We eventually had to figure that issue out after the merger with Trainline. We were now forced to find a new model that worked for the two worlds which had been brought together. So, we introduced new levels across the company. We used the above criteria to make it transparent as to why someone was classed in what level. However, we no longer published the monetary elements alongside the levels. This was a difficult change, but an unavoidable one that we should have made the moment that the transparency we had tried to maintain became a farce. Culture is also about putting the truth out there as it is. You will be surprised how well, even on unpopular matters, honesty will be well received by the teams. And by the way, for me as a German, it always made me feel uncomfortable to speak about salary levels as this is forbidden in any German contract. Therefore, also keep in mind that this can be a sensitive topic when you want to onboard more international colleagues.

However, we did do one thing right that stood and helped to shape a strong culture: we **proactively raised salaries**. That is something that I had not seen in any other company. And it is so powerful when an employer comes to say thank you for great work, and then actively suggests a raise, instead of the employee having to ask for it. I have never seen a more surprised and grateful face than when a team member was told this. It makes people feel so appreciated, and they will become the most loyal teammates you can imagine.

Finally, when we talk about remuneration, we need to cover **how best to distribute bonuses**. Broadly, there are three different ways to do this:

1. Link the entire bonus to the success of the company
2. Link the entire bonus to the success of the individual
3. A combination of both

You want to reward people for their individual success, but not in a way that stands in opposition to the success of the company. The risk with individual bonuses is that they lead to political manoeuvring to achieve individual goals, which is the last thing you need when you want to run fast and achieve results. Therefore, I recommend combining both. And the higher you climb the internal hierarchy, the higher becomes the percentage of both your variable part (50% of your salary is nothing shocking at the top) and the part that is linked to the company's results. But whichever way you choose to do it, a bonus will always only be a reward for the previous year and won't keep someone on board for the following year. However, what can work nicely is the offer to transfer a bonus into **shares**. That encourages people to stay, *and* you keep as much cash in the bank as possible.

Striving for diversity

The final culture topic I wanted to address is **diversity**, as this is, in my view, one that is often discussed the wrong way around. Achieving a more diverse workforce is not about doing anyone a favour or meeting a quota. You do it because it is proven to have a powerful impact on the productivity and creativity of the business, and this will then help you to scale faster. Let me elaborate on two key aspects of diversity that I have seen drive the greatest positive change: A) becoming more international and B) overcoming the gender gap.

A. I decided not to have an extra chapter on **internationalisation**. When you are serious about it, this should be an in-built part of all areas of your company, starting with your teams. As great and enriching as different cultures and languages are, there is a need to acknowledge that they do create the need for an extra effort of communication. At the pace with which your business needs to develop these must not be factors which slow you down. As I have recommended, start by creating an all-English language environment, unless you can say with certainty that you will never have an international colleague, customer or investor, and this becomes one less thing to worry about. It can become super-complicated to change that habit if not implemented from the outset, but once it has been put in place, it is there for good. It can even become a USP of your employer brand, and you will also stop assuming and start listening more carefully to avoid misunderstandings and be mindful of intercultural sensitivities.

B. Tech companies often have very few **women** working in their ranks. That is partly the fault of the tech companies and partly due to women still being extremely underrepresented in tech schools. Until this changes, make sure that women receive privileged treatment when it comes to hiring. I am not saying that you should hire women who are not excellent, but if you have a choice between a man and a woman at the same quality level, choose the woman until your company is at least 50% female at all levels.

The next challenge is to make sure that you pay and develop them at the same pace as their male colleagues, because they might not be as pushy. Therefore, compare their salaries and make adjustments proactively, as described above. Otherwise, the risk is that you have a male top vs a female bottom workforce, which is counterproductive for your culture and simply unfair. Why do I feel so strongly about this topic? Well, we are so far away from a situation where men are underrepresented that I can never see how my own sex could be discriminated against by suggesting bringing in more women. If we ever come close to this, we can have that discussion again, but until then, we need more women in our ranks!

Being in favour of diversity in theory is one thing, but to bring more international staff and more women into the company requires tangible action, which brings us to another important HR topic:

The recruitment and onboarding process

Not being able to bring in and up-to-speed as many new colleagues as you need quickly enough can become a serious bottleneck to your growth. Finding several dozen highly qualified specialists from within the large European start-up hubs is getting increasingly difficult. And it's not a question of money. You need to prepare for this challenge without decreasing your standards or compromising your values. So, what else can you do? Here is my **top-10-list to successfully scaling your recruiting process**:

1. Start by **hiring a recruiter** who is a specialist in the field that you will recruit the most in – for example, a tech recruiter requires a special skillset.

2. Your people are your best ambassadors, so **create an employer brand** around your excellence in recruiting and onboarding, and incentivise internal referrals.

3. **Meet as many superstars as you can** even before you have identified a specific position. Ideally you should aim to clearly have in mind the people you will need during the following 9 months. The best people are the most chased and with the longest notice periods. You need to get to a position where you have at least a couple of choices in your head for every major position you are looking to fill, even before you start officially searching.

4. **Check on the culture-fit** when you select your candidates. Every interview should include specific questions aimed at finding out if there is a match. And from my own experience, if you don't feel right about the person and have doubts, then don't hire that person, even if on paper they are the greatest specialist on the planet. My favourite question to ask in this area is, "What can you add as value that we don't already have?" It's a tough one and will tell you everything you need to know.

5. **Check on motivation**. I know you're in a hurry, but you need highly motivated people, and so I strongly recommend having them submit a case study to test if

they are willing to invest time and energy to secure the job. And this obviously allows you to check on the required skillset at the same time.

6. **Don't democratise your hiring**. In the beginning, everybody gets involved and has a veto. With masses of new positions open, only direct management, direct colleagues and HR should be involved, with the line manager having the final say. Just like the remuneration topic, this change needs to be explained, but the process is otherwise not scalable.

7. Dare to say no and **don't waste time**. Politeness doesn't help the candidate or yourself. When it reads "fluent in English" on a CV and the answer to "What's your name" is "27", stop the process right there. If a person shows up late, it's over before it starts. The recruitment process needs to be efficient, fair and honest on both sides. A favourite moment was when a candidate put German on their CV, didn't do their homework about me and then didn't even understand me saying good morning in German. This was one of my shortest interviews ever, at around 25 seconds, ending on the way into the meeting room.

8. **Bring in more specialists**. The right people and their expertise are key to the maturing process of an organisation. Try to bring in someone from your industry who has that instant recognition of the issues you are trying to solve. They will know where the pain points and boundaries are, and are better able to speak the specific language of your industry. All this will help you greatly in establishing credibility and, ultimately, later in securing the valuation you are seeking.

9. **Make the most of your onboarding**. Be welcoming and open-minded to welcoming your latest hires, to help to bring them up to speed as quickly as possible. This is the first impression you leave with them and sets the bar for your expectation of excellence work- and culture-wise. The greatest feedback we received about our culture from new joiners was that everybody took the time to answer their questions and never made them feel stupid. We all become blind to the things that we deal with every day. Having someone new around is the best thing that can happen to you. Appreciate their objectivity and let them challenge the things you have always done in a certain way. You need a designated person for the onboarding process and set up a procedural checklist to ensure the same high-quality level for all new joiners.

9¾. I was asked and developed an opinion on **whether to recruit family and friends** that I feel like sharing here. For me personally, it was a categoric no, as I tried to separate my private and professional lives as much as possible. I have never recruited people I have considered friends. Whenever things would get complicated, this would make it awkward for both sides, and it wouldn't help the business that pays both our salaries. I have however become close friends with people I have worked with. And I have also seen it work for others. As a rule, I would say that when both parties are OK with it and there is no hierarchical difference between them, I don't think it's an issue. To the contrary, often hiring a friend or sister of someone who has proven to be a cultural fit is a good fit too.

10. **Don't hire with unconscious bias**. We all say we don't and yet we all do. Yes, you too, there are simply no exceptions. When you want to diversify the team to perform better instead of stewing in one's own juices, you need to be open to the new, but that requires training that you and your team should have on a regular basis and which will be checked upon in the due diligence process. Having it now is a double win for you.

Firing

When we speak about recruiting, we also need to speak about the topic that has some of the most flowery descriptive words in English that do their best to disguise what can be a brutal event: "Having to let go", "Making someone redundant". Look, I'm talking about firing. Why is it so demonised and not just seen for what it is: a working relationship coming to an end, because one or both parties are not good for each other anymore. The employee and the business might have developed in different directions and therefore have decided to split.

"Breaking up is never easy, I know", but you owe it to the well-being of the company to act when needed. It shouldn't be done lightly or without rules, as it can be in some regions of the world, but the people I'm referring to in this book are the crème de la crème who will be just fine. I would even go further – you're sometimes doing people a favour in letting them go. Often the reason for an underperformance is simply that they are no longer happy in the position or in the business. The company will change quickly, and it's not a failure for either party to acknowledge that. It was the right person in the right role for a while, and you have gone down a path together which deserves the greatest respect, but it might now be time to move on for both parties. Wish them well in a generous spirit, so that they can remain ambassadors for the company.

My piece of advice is therefore to **face this issue head-on** and do not tiptoe around your decision. I have had to let people go in all positions and companies I have worked with, and I'm still getting birthday cards from some of them. Why is that? Because I treated them with the respect they deserved. And if you have an interest in having them depart as good leavers, then why not let them keep some shares to vest. While you might waive the (very costly) non-compete clause, with your shares in their pocket, they are less likely to show up at your biggest competitor before your exit.

Obviously, **firing should always be the very last option** and one should look thoroughly into any issues and identify development opportunities first. Another important rule is to never fire someone out of a dogmatic stance, just because you disagree with a well-formed opinion. Always let the better argument win, not the hierarchy. However, when someone is no longer aligned on culture or quality, immediate action is required. And when I say immediate, I mean ideally by the end of the week. And that has probably been the single biggest mistake I have made. At times, I have tried to hold on to talented and loyal people for too long, even after there clearly wasn't a cultural fit anymore. By doing so, I not only demotivated them, but everybody around them, forgetting about the other hundred people that I was responsible for. Seeing a separation as a natural option helps to scale faster and, as contradictory as it might sound, as part of the reality of a scale-up, it is sustainably healthier for the culture.

If you are forced to go down the legal road, **be mindful and respectful of the detailed complex procedure** you will need to follow and get yourself some help. Don't let it get messy because you didn't play by the rules. Start by properly documenting performance discussions, ideally being able to prove that the performance issue has been mentioned over several months. This is an area where it is vital to have detailed processes in place to protect you when something goes wrong. And something will go wrong, it's simply a matter of time. Before you start rolling your eyes or skip to the next chapter, let me tell you that, while it's hardly ever love at a first sight, you will be very positively surprised how much you are going to get from implementing the correct organisational structures and processes, I promise!

Organisational structure and processes

This is not about adding unnecessary paperwork where it doesn't make sense. What you need to install are objective instruments so that ideally, no issue can go unnoticed. You need to **start by being able to answer the following 5 questions with a big yes**. If you cannot, then additional processes need to installed *today*.

1. Are managers conducting regular (at least bi-weekly) 1:1s with their team members?
2. Has there been a bi-annual review on performance for every member of the team and has it been documented in writing?
3. Does everybody in your business have a signed job description (JD) including a clear RACI and know what their decision-making power is?
4. Does everybody know from whom and to what amount they can accept gifts? Is annual compliance training being conducted with the whole team?
5. Is a clear and up-to-date organisational chart available for everyone to access at any time?

Unfortunately, many of these things go unnoticed until they explode. These can include – managers not speaking to their teams; compliance rules not being followed; performance expectations not having been clearly documented; or even worse, bullying or harassment. Don't think it can't happen to your business. That is what I thought, and I was wrong.

In the beginning you're this cute little start-up that will be forgiven for not having applied all the regulations properly. After all, you're setting out to break the mould of your sector, you're moving ahead of the established players with your fresh, disruptive thinking. All that procedural and administrative stuff is just going to slow you down and make you more like the old guard. The problem is, all this can come back and bite you once you scale up. When you grow bigger, any degree of tolerance by the authorities and legislators will decrease and finally disappear entirely. And suddenly that large gift you accepted from your client just before the contract signing will land in your lap just at the point when it is a major distraction. And I haven't even mentioned the most important point: it will have an impact on your market valuation. Investors are acutely aware of the importance of **implementing proper processes** and will check on all the detail of this during your DD. Any non-compliance could damage your valuation, derail an acquisition or, in extreme circumstances, kill off the whole project. Everything will depend on how seriously you have put in place the necessary organisational processes to be able to answer all those questions above in the affirmative.

Processes can only work when they are embedded in a functioning organisation, which is not something that just happens but needs shaping so that it can accompany your strategy. It's not about titles, it's about how your teams work together and how information flows so that decisions can be made clearly and efficiently. Personally, I have always been fascinated by organisational behaviour, which to me describes the psychology of a company. When you see it that way, you will happily invest in the right working environment for your fast-growing world.

Like any society, your business needs rules and regulations to coexist, calibrated to ensure they do not hinder creativity, but clear enough and written down to avoid misinterpretations. None of this is about a lack of trust or being risk averse, but especially in times of change, every business needs a guiding map to not get lost on the way. A good tool that helps here is your **organisational chart**. Create this to help you to get ahead of the game in building your world, instead of only reacting to what the world has in store for you. What do you want it to look like in 9- and 18-months' time? If you have a plan for the organisation on those time horizons, it's easier to anticipate potential challenges well in advance. But the org-chart is not only great for the leader. Put yourself in the shoes of a new joiner. When I joined Captain Train, the business was of such a size that I was able to know most of the names and their roles by the end of my first day. But had I been a new joiner during the far larger scale Trainline times, I would have been grateful to see on an org-chart how my role fitted into the bigger picture.

Here are in summary **the 5 principles needed to build a great organisational structure**:

1. **Keep the organisation as flat as possible,** but with no more than 5 direct reports per individual, to ensure good management.
2. **Decisions cannot be taken top down** only but should lie with the experts.
3. **It's not about titles or hierarchy**, it's about guaranteeing the flow of information.
4. **The organisation must follow your strategy** and that needs to be reflected in the staffing of key roles and departments.
5. The role of the **product must remain at the heart of the organisation**, no matter how big you grow.

To bring the above to life, I will show an example of how an organisation can evolve over time. In the beginning you usually start with a classical hierarchical organisation with silo-departments that work next to each other. There is no separation between the functional and the managerial responsibilities. And honestly, to start with, this will do the trick. At Captain Train, we tried to spice it up a bit by turning the hierarchy upside down in the org-chart, with the C-level at the bottom to indicate that managers were service providers to their teams.

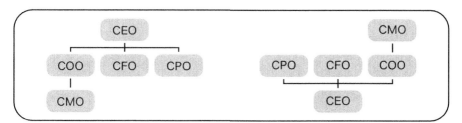

Fig 7: *Classical Organisational Charts*

And then over time, the silo-departments grow and think less and less about customers or the product and more and more about themselves, creating their own agendas. Marketing is doing marketing to do marketing and not to promote the product. Tech is doing tech for their own purposes and not necessarily because it is what the customer wants. Therefore, it's crucial to re-align all departments to the company's objectives during your scaling phase, making sure that everything again spins around the customers and the product.

Here is one example of how you can achieve that: put the product back at the heart of the company by working in clusters, called squads, and separating management from functional responsibilities. The sweet thing about this logic is the extra accountability that is handed over to the squads. Their direct output becomes more tangible and consequently their motivation and commitment will go up. Even better, the whole company will become more results driven. And that's exactly where you want to get to in the "culture pyramid for scale-ups".

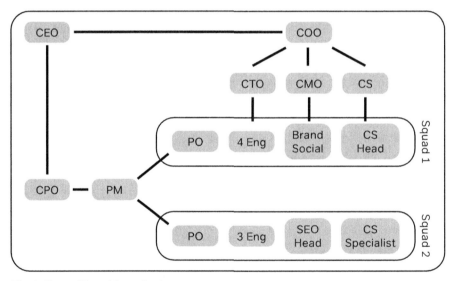

Fig. 8: *Cluster/ Squad Organisation*

However, changing to a squad logic only makes sense for businesses with more than a hundred people and at least a year ahead of an exit, as it takes time to implement and to make the new organisation operate smoothly. What it looks like is best explained using an example: A squad works on opening up China as a new market for the business. To achieve this, the product owner (PO) manages the overall delivery and obviously owns the product roadmap for this project. He has a team made up of:

- three dedicated engineers to work on the product.
- someone from the SEO team to ensure that the content will go live in Mandarin.
- one customer service (CS) resource to serve the Chinese customers in the future.

This is the squad in charge, and as such it can take key decisions within the frame that has been designated for them. However, this does not mean that the PO is their line manager, they "only" hold the functional accountability. The CS specialist is still managed by the head of CS, and the SEO person is still part of the CMO department. Resource planning is then agreed upon higher up the hierarchy. This 'trade meeting' should be steered by product and will decide on how to spend resources across all key strategic initiatives.

The prerequisite for this to work is to trust and accept that your specialists will make the right calls, and that you no longer have every single piece of information outside your squads. If you get to run your organisation in this way, you will have made a great step towards positive scaling, faster and better decision-making, and putting the customers and the product at the heart of all activities.

Development and Training

Being the business coach that I am today, I cannot close an HR chapter without a training and development section. Human resources are also there to serve as a service centre and as a business partner to develop talent on a personal and business level. This support is necessary to the often young and inexperienced start-uppers who are now becoming more mature within the business. The challenge you will find is that they tend to idealize the beginning and react emotionally to changes to that alleged paradise. But it's a human way of articulating the fear of loss and you can guide them by building bridges to the new world and accompany change with coaching, mentoring or training.

Before we continue to talk about details, I have a heads-up to share, because you can also develop people in the wrong direction. A common mistake is to push your highly talented specialists into management responsibility. What if that career path is not for everyone and how does it help the company to have your greatest specialists leading teams and hindering them from executing what they are best at? And what about the teams they lead and the impact on the culture? Therefore, it is essential to acknowledge that making a career should not automatically imply having to take on management responsibilities. The best way is to have two different career paths that are valued the same in the business, one as an expert and another as a manager.

Once you have identified the most appropriate career path, there are crucial differences between coaching, mentoring and training. **Coaching** believes that in general you have everything you need to achieve your goals and it "only" needs structure and articulation. A coach asks questions in a non-directive way, helping you to define your goal, find solutions, chose options and commit to them. The aim is for you to gain altitude to sustainably become more aware of yourself, personally and professionally, to achieve your defined goals. These can range from becoming a better leader to better coping with the tremendous pressure you might be under.

The coach's job is to accompany you on this path, creating a safe space to become your thinking partner. It often involves so-called 360-degree feedback, in which your coach will interview people from all areas around you: your team members, your peers, your superior and, if you wish, even friends or family members, to get the most complete view possible, following a list that you provide. The aim is to get a realistic view on yourself and to discover your blind spots. By the way, this tool works for annual reviews as well. At Trainline, I used that twice a year for my direct reports and asked them to rate themselves as well. The resulting discussions can be very fruitful, and on this basis of that extra dimension of self-analysis, it is much easier to gain agreement on future actions – you should try it! You could start by asking two simple questions:

1. What did X do well during the past 6 months and should do more of?
2. What could X improve or stop doing?

A coach ideally is someone external, whereas a **mentor** can be someone inhouse, a more senior person of the company, sometimes even your boss, and is more of a long-term counsel whom you reach out to on specific work-related issues along your way. If you invest in them sufficiently, these relationships can often last way beyond the actual work relationship. I have a mentor from every company I have worked with and I have been in contact with them ever since. Three of them have become my closest counsels for the past decades and have been invaluable support for me along the way, and one of them, I can call a friend today. And, whenever you feel there is someone worth being supported, reach out and offer *your* mentorship, to pass on the baton.

And, last but not least, there is **training**, as a separate category. When you start a new job, you need specific skills such as how to use a software programme more efficiently, or you may have become a manager for the first time and wonder what that actually requires. All this is not a task for a coach or a mentor but calls for hands-on training. I can only encourage you to proactively ask your HR person about it. Ideally, this should be part of the discussion in every bi-annual review in which you agree on a development plan. Don't see it as a sign of weakness to reach out for support, rather the opposite, it's a healthy sign of a hunger to grow. And here comes the best part: in most European countries, a budget for training is often made available by the state which is hardly ever fully used by the eligible companies.

Developing your key talent should be an anchor in any strong company culture and is key to the success of the business. It needs to start with the founders having a positive attitude towards development and training and then passing this onto the management and finally to the whole team. In a fast-changing world, offering guidance to your teams will make a huge difference to their development. And their development will be your asset.

Personally, I negotiated coaching into my contract whenever I made a larger move, and certainly when it implied more leadership responsibility. And my company rightly required me to attend management seminars before I could take over my first team. Unfortunately, it is still a very European mindset to consider that all learning has been done by the time we leave school or college, whereas in America continuing education has been an accepted thing for a long time. In times when new tech is changing the world every other day, we all are likely to change careers many times during our working lives. As a result, we should revaluate our attitude and appreciate that even within the lifespan of our business, we will need to reinvent ourselves at least a couple of times. Personal development and training can be a guarantor and accelerator to do so with success.

TOP 3
Takeaways

1. Hire an HR head and start documenting and thinking in organisational structures

2. Put your culture at the heart of everything you do, and develop your high potentials

3. Set up a working recruiting and onboarding process that allows you to go fast and let go asap of people that become poison for the culture

CHAPTER 5

The Role that has No Peers

This second people chapter is the one that I've been looking forward to writing the most. It explores the role of the CEO and its impact on ensuring that your scale-up becomes a success. It is also somewhat about my professional life over the past decade where I have held this role myself. I will discuss issues around leadership and management and whether being the CEO is a position you can grow into or if it simply requires a specific set of qualities as prerequisites that you either have or you don't. I never felt the weight of big budgets on my shoulders, but every day, I was acutely aware of the responsibility I had for my team. I understood that my actions could have an impact on so many aspects of their lives, from whether they liked coming to work to even whether they would be spending a contented evening after work with their loved ones.

But this is not simply a chapter from a CEO aimed solely at a CEO. It is really for everybody who is a leader or wants to become one, be it for a team or a project. And even if you have decided that leadership is not for you, this chapter will still help you to better understand where your boss comes from and what drives them. This has a value for you and for the business, as you will be able to work out how best to support each other. It is often said that you join a company for its culture but leave because of your manager. I am confident that this won't happen to anyone who takes in the following pages.

We need to acknowledge that leadership in the start-up and scale-up world is a highly specific challenge. Often, its leaders have started young, and their first or second attempt to create a business might have failed. And then it may well be that now, a third attempt has worked out. Even in that scenario it is relatively overnight that you find yourself alone in front of a large team or project and are expected to know how to lead.

Unlike in the corporate world, with hundreds of leaders, in a scale-up, a single mediocre leader can break the entire machinery. On top of not being equipped for it, you may have never had a manager as a role model to learn from and develop your own style. The success of the business is dependent on its leader. So, investing in yourself as a leader and manager, and investing in ensuring great leaders and managers are in place, carries a tremendously high ROI and therefore should always be a key priority. What makes this even more important is that you are more likely to experience rough patches during the scaling phase. More than that, and I have experienced this, you are likely to have at least one moment of terror where you believe that your business won't make it. However, it is at those moments that everything rests on you. You are in charge, and it is critical for the business that you are capable of being at your best in these situations. Surfing on the wave of success is the easy part. It is those moments of facing up to and surviving an existential threat to the business when true superstars are born. Overcoming such a baptism of fire then increases the likelihood of being able to make it across the finishing line. Luckily, CEOs of scale-ups are known for their fighting attitude, and so, if you grow your leadership and management qualities, there is no reason why you won't be able to make it.

Before we dive into this emotive subject, we should start by clarifying what we mean by **leadership and management**. What both tools have in common is that they are equally important for a CEO to succeed in their role. But how are they different from each other? While I have read tons of definitions, my all-time favourite one is a quote from Alexander den Heijer, which reads:

> "When I talk to managers, I get the feeling they're important. When I talk to leaders, I get the feeling I am important."

This has stuck with me, because it articulates beautifully that ability of a leader to inspire others and have people follow them voluntarily, whereas a manager gets people to work for them by executing their hierarchical power.

The qualities of a leader

I believe that there are two kinds of people – those who see the world as it is and those who see the world as it could be one day. The latter can visualise a potential future so clearly that they drive relentlessly to getting there, thus making it a reality. Casting this vision and being able to articulate it so vividly that you bring others with you on your journey is the most important quality of a leader. You move ahead because you have a plan which others are keen to follow, because they believe in it and in you to lead them there. I always compare a leader to being the captain of a large ship, who doesn't have to use their rank to force people onboard but achieves this through their strong communication skills. Potential crew members will want to know what the destination is, how long the journey will take, where they will be sleeping and if there is enough food. Most importantly though, they need to feel that they can trust the captain to get them there safely. It is only once the captain has been recognised as being honest, readable and reliable that everyone will come on board and be convinced that they want to be part of this trip of a lifetime. They will all now come aboard highly committed and energetic, even if the voyage is into unknown territory. This is something only **great leadership** can achieve.

However, let's clarify a common misunderstanding – leadership is not about making everybody happy, or else I would have opened a chocolate store instead. On the contrary, it involves speaking some uncomfortable truths honestly and openly when necessary. I have conducted extremely heated discussions on controversial positions I have held in all-company meetings. But not having these would have compromised my credibility and left the issues unsolved. While you might lose popularity points on a personal level, confronting and resolving potentially negative topics is likely to make you be respected even more as a leader. In a rough sea, your team needs to know that the captain will tell them honestly and openly when there is an iceberg ahead, and ideally early enough to avoid a collision.

In relation to this metaphor, I have seen quite a number of bad managers in scale-ups, but nowhere else have I seen more amazing leaders. The only thing they had been missing to achieve their full leadership potential had been great communication skills. People wanted to follow because they intuitively felt that the leader had a ground-breaking vision. However, they couldn't see the picture as clearly as the leader could because this vision had not been clearly articulated. Therefore, as a reminder, the **top-three-things that every leader should constantly be doing are**:

1. Be **clear on your vision** and write it down/visualise it for others to understand.

2. **Take people on the journey with you** and align them with you through communication, inspiration and motivation.

3. Be transparent on **where you stand on the way** to your destination. There might be changes of direction in between, but embrace the change and innovate, explaining the reasons along the way.

Let me share one personal eye-opening story that I find to be representative for most scale-ups. Just like many of you right now, I was trying my best to be a good leader day-in and day-out. I invested tons of times and tried to be the best version of myself. But on the other hand, I never thought that would make much of a difference really. That changed one day once and for all: after a shortened night, when I had a fever, I came to work in the morning and felt like I hadn't even woken up yet. I tried to sneak into my office and close the door to hide away. On the way, I went past a couple of people from my team, tried to smile and continued on my suffering way and made it into my office. Literally 3 minutes later, my assistant showed up at my door, extremely worried, asking me what was wrong. Apparently, Slack was exploding, and people were worried, not because I was sick, but because rumours were already circulating that we would be shutting down the office. I looked at her in disbelief, until I worked out that it must have been linked to the way I had greeted people that morning. It just wasn't like me, I hadn't been sending out any of my usual energy, I wasn't positive, I wasn't caring, and they had never seen me like that before. And that was the moment when I understood how important my role was and that I could make a positive impact by being a great leader. I didn't take myself more seriously after this incident but, to avoid any similar misinterpretation, the next time I felt sick like that, I worked from home.

I hope that I have convinced you that leadership is important and that it can make a difference. Following on from that, my next question for you is, what kind of leader do you want to be? Theories vary on there being anything from 3 right up to 12 different leadership styles, with 7 apparently being the new consensus. My personal definition includes the following 6:

1. **Autocratic:** A leader who takes decisions without consulting the team and just insists on how things are to be done.
2. **Transactional:** Results-driven, through a combination of rewards and sanctions.
3. **Transformational:** Develops a clear vision and as a leader acts and behaves as a role model to encourage desired behaviour.
4. **Coaching:** Believes in the talent of their teammates and lets them take decisions.
5. **Democratic:** Constantly involves the whole team in every decision.
6. **Laissez-faire:** No supervision at all, the opposite of autocratic.

Personally, I place myself somewhere between the transformational and the coaching style. Even back when I was in executive roles at organisations, before I became a business coach, I saw that the coaching style drove the best results for my teams. Conversely, the democratic style didn't work for me while the business grew, and the laissez-faire and autocratic styles I soon came to realise were too extreme and ill-suited for scale-ups. As you can see in the 'Leadership Models in Scale-Ups' diagram below, leadership style can and should evolve over time and, interestingly enough, in the same pattern in all start- and scale-ups I have been involved with. What should remain constant is your authenticity and your appreciation for people. However, the closer you get to the exit, in an increasingly results-driven environment, the more transactional your leadership style will need to become in order to reach the finish line.

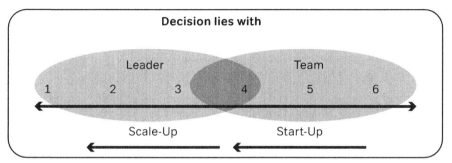

Fig 9: *Leadership Models in Scale-Ups*

Being an effective manager

Once you have used your qualities as a leader to cast the vision, you need a way to apply and deliver against it. This is where **management** comes into the picture. The *Cambridge Dictionary* defines managing as: "To succeed in doing or dealing with something, especially something difficult". You need to break down the vision into tangible deliverables, using your hierarchical power to implement a structure and a budget in line with your strategy. However, being a good manager is not entirely different from being a good leader. You first need to have a plan and then be prepared for it to change, ensuring you take your teams with you along the way. A manager does focus more on details though, and while you should trust your teams to deliver at that granular level, you need to monitor and care about the specifics of their output. For me, the objective of management during a scale-up, in one sentence, is to put in place a framework and guidance that brings out the best in people in this ever-changing environment.

Again, there are different styles of management, but they don't evolve as much over the phases of a scale-up, so that is why I am ignoring them in this book. You are well enough equipped with the leadership style discussion. The most important thing as a manager, just as with a leader, is authenticity throughout the whole adventure, so that your teams feel at ease with you in that role. That's why I think that the best way to give you some food for thought is to share my personal maxims on management:

- **Explain how you operate:** From the outset, I have always sat down with the people I have worked closely with, to talk about my expectations and to listen to theirs. For example, I have ensured that they know that a short email from me, ignoring any salutation, isn't intended to be rude, but simply saves time in amongst an avalanche of emails. If there was a specific issue, they could expect that I would bring it to the table. Until then, they could trust me that all was working well. But I was crystal clear that I expected on-time delivery in the agreed quality, unless I heard in advance that there might be a roadblock that I could help with. And finally, I laid out what good management meant for me and what I expected from my direct reports in their roles as managers.

- **Be readable and consistent** in everything you do. A bad day for you can't become a bad day for them by you choosing to pass this on to your teams simply because you are feeling the pressure. Stability will help your teams to be more productive. Whatever happens, try to be a reliable business partner in all kinds of situations.

- You need to **trust your people and show integrity**. Don't tell them how to do their job. Instead, work out their deliverables, and provide them with the right information and tools. Coach them on how to get there by being a sparring- and thinking partner for them. Empower them by delegating and avoid micromanaging. To hold them accountable, avoid bypassing them by intervening with their direct reports. And when there is an issue in their teams, you bring it to the table with your directs and let them solve it. Your role is to keep their backs free from any potential issue, so that they can concentrate on delivering the agreed results.

- Set clear KPIs, **involving your directs in the planning**, so that they identify with them and own them entirely.

- **Anticipate change** and have plans B and C ready, while delivering all of the above. That can be developing an alternative client, a budget component, or potentially replacing someone in your team.

- **Work on your structure:** Make sure you have the right people and organisation to achieve your goals. As explained, in a fast-changing environment you should revisit this point on a regular basis. The structure and the team you worked with last year might have been the perfect match, but when the whole world around you has changed, maybe your organisation needs to as well.

- There is **nothing more important than your direct reports**. Respect the regular 1:1 slot, and when they urgently need you, make time within the day. Always.

The 1:1 meeting really is the most important meeting for every manager. Making the most of it is key to being a good manager, and that is why I thought, as an ideal model for most meetings, I would share my thoughts on my multiplication formula on how to conduct 1:1s most effectively:

- **Objective:**
    - Find out how they are doing.
    - How can you be of help to empower them on any likely roadblocks?
    - Where do they stand vs the plan?

- **Framework:**
    - 30 minutes max. What you can't cover in half an hour, you won't be able to cover at all. If there is something bigger, you should set up a separate session on that topic.
    - Hold at least every second week.
    - Preparation is key: exchange topics in a shared drive and have them send a final agenda a day in advance.
    - Let them guide you through the 1:1. They are in charge.
    - Documentation is key. Your direct report should send out minutes of the meeting afterwards that you follow up on at the beginning of the next session.

- **My two favourite questions that usually bring up everything you need to know:**
    - How are you doing on a scale from 1 to 10?
    - What can I do to get you to a solid 10?

Over time, your team gets bigger, and with every 0 added to the team size, the topics that end up on your desk become more and more abstract. At one point, I remember I had to decide on things I had never heard of before. But not to worry, with more experience on how you come to decisions, you will know whom to ask to get the relevant information. Consequently, it will become just another milestone in your management range. That is why it is so important to apply scalable processes for yourself and understand how you operate most efficiently in the early days, so that you are less likely to struggle with the challenges of a growing team. Ideally, you should never have more than five direct reports at any point – it is then just the organisation below which gets bigger. Start by becoming less operational and delegate more, as depicted in the below 'Operational-Hierarchy Diagram'. I know it can be hard to break the hands-on pattern, but unless you do, you will destabilise the company and won't be able to focus on where you add most value.

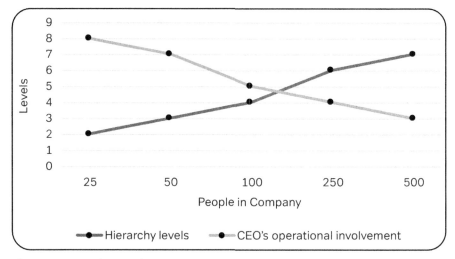

Fig 10: *Operational-Hierarchy Diagram*

The role of the CEO: A leader and a manager

In summary, a CEO's success will depend on being both an outstanding leader and a good manager at the same time. Because even when the CEO decides to hire a COO at some point to manage the operational part of the company on their behalf, they still need to manage that person and the stakeholders also. A CEO will always have to be a manager too. Period.

But there are other elements too that fall under the **role of the CEO**. And while your agenda becomes increasingly busy and hectic, with more and more time spent speaking to (potential) investors, it's important to be mindful of what you should focus on, with the company needing to continue to operate smoothly. As a rule of thumb, CEOs should be working on the things where they add most value and that nobody else can take over from them.

To be more specific on these elements, I suggest that you write the **CEO's job description (JD)**, even if it's your own. This is a great exercise to undertake and then to use to compare with what you do spend your time on. The following is not your precise JD obviously, but a general overview of all the tasks that all CEO JDs I have seen have in common.

I would start with something like: The CEO is the most senior employee of the company (founder or not), who is…

- A **leader to the whole team**, casting and communicating the vision to inspire the team to follow.
- The **Chief Cultural Officer** who initiates and leads the company's culture during change.
- **Puts in place the right structure** (organisational chart) and internal communication to deliver against strategy, vision and mission.
- A **manager to his direct team**: recruiting, empowering and developing the execs to deliver against their team OKRs (Objectives and Key Results) and the company's KPIs (Key Performance Indicators).
- The **face of the company**: external ambassador and spokesperson, as well as increasingly involved in investor relationships and fundraising.
- **Most senior key account manager** for your largest customers' most senior partners. (In my experience, even as president, it was regularly me who spoke to the CEOs of the railway industry. Be it in the beginning to set the framework, in between when the deal got stuck somewhere on the way or in the end to close the deal.)
- In charge of the **board and the stakeholder management**.

Invest in stakeholder management and in your board

On this last point, the importance of **investing in stakeholder management**, other start- and scale-uppers have often disagreed with me and considered this a waste of time. My response to them is that it's only a waste of time when it's not managed properly, and it will become a key element of your role when your ambitions are to achieve a successful exit. That's why I'm going to zoom in here, to show you how you can get the most out of this underrated topic.

Let's start by admitting that it is politics that I'm talking about. The more external funds you accept, the more powerful your board will become, and you need to counterbalance that. What you want to achieve is to have your board members working for you and to use them to achieve your objectives. To get there, you need them to trust you. You will have experienced professionals on your board who will have played this game many times before. Ignoring this on your side could end up breaking your neck. On the other hand, when playing along, it will add great value and even become good fun – after all, who doesn't love to win a good game?

The first step to effective stakeholder management (not only for the CEO) is to be clear on who your key stakeholders are. It is not just your board members. What helped me to see this clearly was drawing up a **stakeholder mind-map** for myself. Picture yourself as an octopus – you're the head in the middle, the commando centre. Your tentacles reach out for all the information that you can pass on from one arm to the other to test and learn how others will respond. Using your stakeholders as a sounding board will help you to build up a more complete view and to encounter healthy challenges to your strategy and the way you operate. From all this, you will soon establish a clear view about who you will receive the most precious input from or who will be giving you the most challenges. These are the people you need to be in closest contact with.

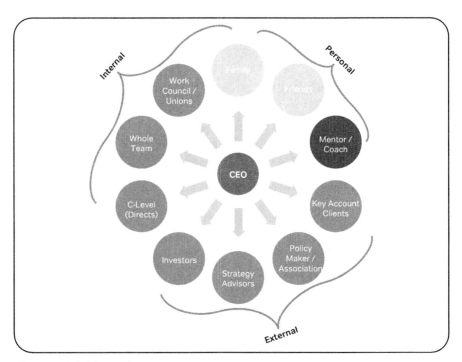

Fig 11: Stakeholder Mind-Map

The above is an example of my personal mind-map as CEO, which includes internal, personal and external parties. I covered internal stakeholders earlier and will speak about your personal ones later in this chapter, so for now, let's focus on the external ones.

The good news is that they are mostly organised together as boards except when working with policy makers. The latter I will discuss separately and throughout the marketing and exit chapters when talking about lobbying and thought leadership. At this point I will just say this: you should seriously consider bringing someone into your own ranks to influence policy making on your behalf.

But back to championing your board: while you can have investors and advisors on the same board, obviously you would need a different format for one that includes your customers. It's important to get every aspect of your board format correct from the outset, which will help you immensely throughout the process of stakeholder management.

External stakeholders		Managed in (format)
Investors	→	Company board
Strategic advisors	→	Advisory board
Key account clients	→	Customer board
Policy makers/ associations	→	Thought leadership sessions

I have chaired hundreds of board meetings myself, and these days I now sit on the other side, as an appointed non-executive director. It took me a while in my first business to install a professional board which was scalable, and which could help me to achieve my goals, but eventually I got there. Let me share with you how I did it.

The earlier you begin, the easier and more successful it will become over time. Don't start this process just before an exit, as there is a danger at that point that your board will take this out of your hands, if they see that you are unable to manage the situation. The **top-5-elements that a great board should include** to make it function in line with your objectives are:

1. **A regular schedule and participants**: Board meetings should take place every 3 months, with dates blocked long in advance, and remain fixed as much as possible. The board should include you as CEO and chairman, although a third person might take over the chairmanship role at a mature point of the business. Also, at least one other executive (ideally the CFO and COO) and, depending on your size at the beginning, 2-3 investors and non-executive independent advisors sitting in. In the end, expect your large investors to impose 2-3 seats for themselves alone.

2. **A fixed agenda:** Ensure that the duration is never longer than 3 hours. The agenda should always include a CEO- and financial update against the KPIs. Always add a marketing and product section, as you will be challenged on this anyway. Share your board pack at least 48 hours before the meeting to allow for proper preparation.

3. **Short minutes:** These should focus on decisions and action points and be taken by someone from your team (or later a company secretary or general council). They should be distributed no later than a couple of days after the meeting. To be approved at the beginning of the next session.

4. **Don't ask open questions**. Instead, keep greater control by laying out a defined range of options along with recommended actions. Otherwise, you will get lost in discussions. Treat the board as a forum for approving your strategy rather than asking them for advice only. It is therefore important to have any potentially complicated discussions upfront with relevant individuals.

5. The spirit of the meetings should be **positive and honest**, as you do need to know what they really think. Even when they are annoyed, providing them with the opportunity to speak their minds can serves as a catalyst, and it is sometimes sufficient to just let them blow off steam and this enables you to react to this.

By implementing these boards, you show strong leadership with your key external stakeholders, all helping to bring them on the journey with you. And there are other advantages: Firstly, it forces you to report back and adhere to regular milestones to build up some pressure for yourself, that a CEO wouldn't have otherwise. Also, documenting decisions, budgets and salaries in the minutes help you to resign from personal liability and compliance-related issues and quasi automatically prepares your next due diligence perfectly smoothly. Finally, you are creating a trusting relationship that you can count on when things get messy, and I bet my last shirt that this day will come.

Make time for CEO duties

Now, with this overview of stakeholder management, the description of a CEO's role is complete, and you hopefully have a clearer view on where you should be focusing your energy. However, with everything else on your plate that is easier said than done. Therefore, I have developed a **top-10-list of dos and don'ts to free up your time and**

mind space. You might find these useful in helping you to focus, deliver, and add the most possible value against your key tasks:

1. **Become less operational**: Yes, your business tries to disrupt and thrives on creative chaos in all areas, but when the business grows (up), this can't be your prevailing focus anymore. As you get closer to the finish line, you need to step back from operational topics or you risk destabilising the rest of the team.

2. To get there, you need to **delegate** and pass on ownership (move from "R" to "A" in the RACI on most topics), and let the experts take the decisions. However, this does not mean that you shouldn't continue to get involved and challenge opinions.

3. From a start- to a scale-up, all CEOs will need to **remove themselves from most operational responsibilities** before reaching the finish line. In no chronological order, you will need to hire a Chief Product Officer (CPO) and a Chief Operating Officer (COO) to divest management responsibility of all the operational business units. Embrace that change to free up your time and then look to complete your exec team with a Chief Marketing Officer (CMO) and then, before you exit, a Chief Revenue Officer (CRO) or a VP Growth. No matter what title you choose for yourself, installing these positions all sends the same signal: you're ready to scale big time now.

4. Don't be afraid to **get an assistant early** – 100 people is not too small. It's not snobby to get help with administrative stuff to free up your time to grow the business faster and focus on where you add most value. You're doing the business a favour.

5. Don't be the showstopper. See yourself as a **juggler who tries to keep all balls in the air**. You should never drop a ball, and a topic should never be blocked on your desk for a long time, or you hinder others to advance things from their side.

6. Be bold, move fast, **take decisions, and stand by them**. Sometimes it's easier to go for it and apologise later, instead of asking for permission. Either way, stick to your guns, unless you learn some revolutionary news on why it wasn't the right move in the first place.

7. **Be associative** and involve your workforce. By involving a selected group that represents the whole team and deciding together, you can hold them accountable. For example, if you proactively create a work council, instead of waiting to be forced

to install one by law, they will be more likely to thank you by acting as promoters of your cause.

8. **Appreciate feedback and cut to the chase**. Do this by building trust and showing your teams that honest feedback is appreciated and has no negative consequences. They will stop tiptoeing around and put the truth on the table, which can save you precious time.

9. Maintain a **list of your top people** that you want to keep. Nurture these selected individuals to decrease the risk of losing them and avoid unnecessary friction.

10. **Use internal communication to ease the flow of information and avoid unnecessary meetings**. Implement and host all-hands/town-hall style meetings. These, plus your programme of regular 1:1s are crucial to make sure that your information flows down most efficiently. But also ensure that this flow is two-way. Listen and respond to input and feedback from across the business. At the same time, don't fall too in love with meetings though! Don't be afraid to disband meetings where the same things are being said more than once or an email would do the trick instead.

The power of internal communication

Point 10, a focus on **internal communication**, sounds obvious, but is hardly ever taken seriously enough, even though it should be one of a CEO's main concerns. Together with the People head, this should be treated as one of your most powerful tools to make sure that the entire company is aligned on your vision and your strategy, but also on all other major topics that come along unannounced. It further helps to create routines and to structure everyone's work week, month and even year, to show appreciation, increase transparency and give and take feedback more regularly.

When I was a CEO, I prepared for myself an overview of all internal communication that was available to me, and I share this below. It is separated into the manager's role to the C-team and in the leader's role to communicate the vision and taking the temperature of the whole team to make sure that everybody is moving in the desired direction together.

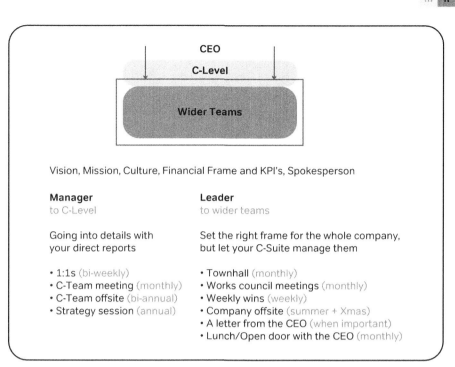

Fig 12: *Internal communication tools for a CEO*

In a growing organisation, you will need to structure your internal communication with some ground rules to keep it effective. Start by formalising communication channels and meetings. For example, I insisted that Slack messages that went out to more than one person were not considered official communication, and I refused to read emails where I was in cc. I didn't win popularity awards for these announcements, but this helped everyone to become more aware of which communication channel was most effective for a specific purpose, and ensured that proper documentation procedures were followed.

On the meeting side, I insisted on being clear on the purpose of the meeting and checked whether it was absolutely necessary. Let me pick a positive example: why are we hesitating to celebrate success or have offsite team-building events that we wrongly declare as strategy meetings? It is so much better to have lunch together offsite and play an escape game, as an incredibly useful exercise that will make your team work more effectively. Go for it, don't disguise it. A meeting can only meet the participant's expectations when they know what they came for.

You don't have to be alone in all this

Now there actually is an **11th point** on how to free up your time and get more mind space in your CEO role. One that is so vital that I have dedicated this separate part of the chapter to it: **surround yourself with the right people**.

Nobody is ever properly prepared to be a CEO, and, as the title of this chapter suggests, a CEO has no colleagues. For some confidential topics you can go internal to exchange views with your HR head, chief of staff or assistant. They know you and the company, they play on your team and can be a great source of feedback for you. However, there are topics that are too confidential, negative or personal. You would scare them and lose your credibility as a leader if you share these with anyone in your team. And yet, you don't have to be alone in this – it is not a sign of weakness to reach out for support. Frankly, I have never seen a CEO succeed in this lonely position without gathering the right people around. You need others to exchange views and ideas, gain perspective, receive honest feedback and benefit from their experience.

As this should not be those from within, you need to create your own kick-ass set of external people to help you out here. Luckily, it's you who gets to choose them. My main piece of advice is to look for people who are not afraid to tell you the truth and have something that you don't: different experience or age profile, or alternative ways of thinking. That obviously requires you to invite them to be open with you and stand criticism. I have a negative example from somebody who didn't that has shaped me ever since. A CEO of a company I once worked for learned from the press that he had been fired, because nobody around him dared to tell him the truth. I swore to myself to never make that same mistake and to surround myself with people who can and will be open and honest with me, even if this would be uncomfortable for me at times. So, who are these wonderful people you should turn to, and where to find them?

- The most important ones for me were my **friends and family**. If my wife had judged me for crazy working hours, or my friends for not calling them in a while, I wouldn't have made it over the finish line. They were and always will be my source of energy and inspiration, the place where I can just *be*, not as a CEO, but as a friend, husband or father.

- Find **people like yourself**. It helps to feel understood to be with current or former CEOs from other scale-ups or from the same industry going through similar experiences. However, as you won't be challenged much, make sure that you have other sources of support too.

- Use your board, especially your **independent advisors**, who have no other interest than serving you as a sounding board to help you succeed. Tell them what you have in mind or have experienced. In most cases, they have been through something similar and exchanging views helps to put things into perspective. I remember reaching out to one of my board members , sharing that I felt like a failure because a bunch of people had left the company after a merger. And I recall how relieved I was to learn that this was totally the norm and something to be expected at that stage of the company. Being in that role myself today, I encourage you to use us as much as you can, and that to do so is a sign of strength.

- Find yourself long-term **mentors and be coached**. I have spoken about the positive impact this can have on your own development. Identify and put in place your personal thinking partner, who is dedicated to securing your wellbeing and success and can create a safe environment for you. I have often seen close and long-term relationships built out from this.

Have you got what it takes?

The final part of this chapter, is an attempt to answer a question I am asked regularly, especially from scale-up CEOs on the verge of giving up: **Do I have what it takes to be the CEO**, or is this just not for me? Let's start with an academic approach to this question by looking at a set of qualities and characteristics that most CEOs have. Among many profile and personality tests, the MBTI (Myers Briggs Type Indicator) is still the most prominent one, looking at 4 opposite pairs:

- **I**ntroversion vs. **E**xtraversion
- **S**ensing vs. **IN**tuition
- **T**hinking vs. **F**eeling
- **J**udging vs. **P**erceiving

With every individual having a unique set, you have a total of 16 possible personality types. And here comes the shocking news: from my experience, there actually is a common CEO profile, which is "ENTJ – Extrovert, Intuitive, Thinking and Judging". While I was a CEO, my personal test result confirmed that profile too. But before you now disaffectedly leave your CEO position to someone else, because you have discovered you have a different profile, relax, it is only a reflection of learned behaviour. That hadn't been my profile when I became a CEO, but the role then shaped my profile. And even today, only a few years out of my last CEO role, I have changed to an "ENFJ" already and, expecting to feel most comfortable in my new role, I see myself being an "ESFJ" in the near future. So, in a nutshell, it might help to start off with a certain profile, but it's not a showstopper.

However, some other things can be major issues: authenticity, charisma, caring for people and being able to express empathy are complicated to learn. Then again, why would you want to become a CEO in the first place, if you don't appreciate leading people? Then there are things that will most definitely help, but can be learned, like having a fallibility with numbers, not having great self-confidence or not feeling comfortable speaking in front of people. You can become better at all these over a period of time, provided you care about them and invest some time in them. I have seen several CEOs who, at the beginning, hated the speaking element but just a year later, with proper media training, found themselves enjoying owning the stage.

By the way, not a prerequisite at all, as is so often falsely claimed, is being able to get away with 3 hours' sleep a night. The sheer number of hours does not give an indication of how well-rested you are or the state of your energy levels. What you need instead is to be prepared to work intensively and flexibly and, as discussed previously, use your time efficiently by finding your own rhythm and charging stations.

If you have read this section so far and are thinking to yourself that this doesn't sound like you at all, especially around the people part, you need to be honest with yourself right now: not all entrepreneurs are made to be the CEO, and some do their businesses a favour by stepping back from that task to let others lead in making it the greatest possible success. Again, this would not be a sign of weakness, but a smart move, shaping the future success for your business. However, if you do recognise in yourself these values and appreciate that leadership and management are crucial elements to your success, and you are willing to learn, there is no reason why you shouldn't become a top executive all the way.

What other qualities can help you to become a top-notch scale-up CEO? The most essential ones are resilience and stamina, although these are not to be confused with stubbornness, dogmatically running into a wall. No, what I mean is not to let the trillion unexpected issues you are going to encounter on your path break you. Stay calm, learn from them, carry on and understand that manoeuvring around them to clear the way for the business and the teams is an important part of your role. I have seen cases where the last person standing became the CEO, because everyone else had surrendered. You need to prepare for a long and bumpy ride.

And last but not least, you should appreciate that the CEO job is not one in which you will receive a lot of positivity from your teams. If you don't hear back from them, take this as a good sign. When there is something wrong, they will let you know. I once had an interim assistant who came to me crying after the first day and said that she hated looking at my mailbox, because there was absolutely nothing positive in there. Other than the fact that she obviously wasn't the right person for the job, it also helped me to realise that I didn't feel that way at all. On the contrary, I relished being the one to find solutions to problems, being the facilitator and consequently implementing sustainable changes. That's how I felt that I could make a difference and add value. I also tried turning the ship around by giving more positive feedback, which changed the whole dynamic. But either way, you need to be intrinsically wired positively, as your job will be to manage from crisis to crisis without the ship sinking.

If this sounds hard – it is! There have been moments when I too was close to giving up and surrendering. I sometimes felt like I just couldn't take it anymore: the pressure and the burden of the huge responsibility I had to carry, combined with the uncertainty of when it is going to end, and even if it's going to pay out at all. Often, I would have to get up at 4 in the morning to catch another early train or flight, knowing that it was going to be another day ahead of difficult negotiation meetings. All the while my mailbox would be overflowing, and there would be at least three other emergencies to deal with at the same time. Sometimes it became more than I could take, while having to put on hold important parts of my private life. And yet, I stayed in the game for eleven consecutive years. And most of the time, I really loved it. What helped me was to find the necessary perspective and to grow personally into my task, applying the exercises that I have talked about. They helped me to find ways to get motivated again and stay positive to appreciate the ride more. And to survive in the C-level of a scale-up, you will need to find yours.

That is why I want to close this chapter by sharing my **3 highlights that worked to help me stay positive**. I hope you can apply one or more of these elements for yourself, and please let me know if you find something else to add:

1. **I don't take things personally**. Negativity is rarely about you as a person. Clearly distinguish between the role that you represent (thinking about the overall wellbeing of the company and its people) and you as a person. When you accept that feedback is about the hat you wear and not your face, you will be able to sleep better and feel less under attack.

2. **I love to see others succeed**, and I see their success as my success. Consequently, I find great pleasure in helping them to set the right framework, so that they can overachieve all expectations. Ideally, they are in fact all smarter and better than you in what they do, but crucially they may well not be better at your CEO job and that should ensure that you can remain confident.

3. **I don't make my age a topic**. I was only 29 when I became a CEO for the first time and was often mistaken for my assistant, causing the funniest situations. But it never bothered me, and unless I made it a topic, my age never was a problem for anybody else either, which is another great example of how autosuggestion can help to put you in the right mindset.

TOP 3
Takeaways

1. Develop a vision and a leadership style that make your team want to follow you

2. Focus on where you can add the most value as a CEO

3. Successful leaders surround themselves with external thinking partners

CHAPTER 6

You're Not Building it for Yourself

I f we see the last couple of chapters as discussions on developing soft skills, this one is all about creating the hardware. No other topics are as passionately discussed in start- and scale-ups as the ones around tech and product, as these are the backbone of any digital business. And while I have only met a handful of people who understood fully what it means to create a world-class product, everybody has a view on it. In that sense, it might help that I'm not part of that elite, in that I'm only half an engineer and have never coded a single line in any of the companies I've been involved with. And yet, I have had CTOs report into me and have successfully led scaling and growth in tech heavy businesses.

There is no doubt that great tech and product are key to most successful start- and scale-ups, but they do not serve a purpose on their own. Having a marvellous product that is still not used by your customers won't make for a successful exit. I am therefore looking at the subject of this chapter completely agnostically. My driver is only ever to create a platform that can scale and can be embedded into the business as a whole, while developing a great product that will be successful in new markets and with all target customer groups.

Create one scalable platform

A good starting point is to look at it from a meta level. Most digital e-commerce marketplaces look something like **the platform** below, combining the front- and the back-end. This is where the magic happens around the data. Data first arrives in the platform in a pure, raw form. Let's compare it to oil, which comes in as a raw material. Picture your platform as the refinery, in which the oil needs to undergo complex and multiple treatment processes to be distilled, converted and stored. What comes out on the other side to consume is the finest petrol. This is precisely what should happen on your platform, to make your customer use your product instead of that of your competitors. You use raw data and add all kinds of value and cool features that nobody else can: languages, currencies and the most up-to-date payment and delivery options. You are creating a whole new, gloriously simple customer experience as output and are striving to set a new standard of excellence. For digital native companies especially, the quality of your platform and the quantity of data that flows through it will determine a fair part of your valuation.

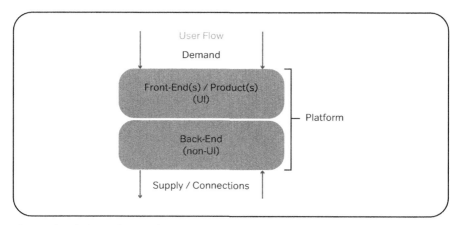

Fig 13: *The Platform of a Digital Business*

Back-End

Let's look at the two pieces of the platform in greater detail, starting at the bottom with the back-end, the part that has no User Interface (UI). This is all about what happens behind the scenes, where the data is processed. In my oil analogy, this would be where the data would be refined. This process can take different shapes. In travel tech and other historically grown industries, you receive your supply by plugging into an inventory of the incumbents that you are trying to disrupt. It's kind of a "coopetition", where you compete and cooperate at the same time, as you are trying to replace only parts of the services offered by the incumbents but still need them as your partner.

However, there are differences in the way the back-end needs to be built out across different industries and businesses. There is the one as described above that is used by Trainline or Booking.com and then there are slight variations, as exemplified by, for example, FlixBus, where their supply comes from their own branded busses and trains that are operated by licensed partners. And then there are different models like streaming services such as Spotify or Netflix, where their supply comes in the form of music or video content. Finally, there are services like Tinder that use network effects. Here, the customer provides the incoming (supply equivalent data) by looking for a partner and waits to be matched at the same time.

Regardless of what your business model might be however, your customers demand a smooth payment experience to purchase your subscription, product or service in their choice of local payment mode in the front-end. This is where you can add a huge amount of value and decrease the complexity for your customers. No matter what happens behind the scenes in the back-end, the customer should experience the same smooth and harmonised booking process in the front-end. That's why you need to invest in integrating a great Payment Service Provider (PSP) like Adyen in the back-end. On the upside, once implemented, future developments on the payment side will be mostly taken care of by them and then automatically made available to you.

The most common scale-up killer is to **limit future integrations or after-sales possibilities**. Think ahead and, from the beginning, allow limitless integrations of all kinds. Think outside the box and reflect on what potential buyers may require, now and at any point in the future. This will increase your chances of a successful exit. Find the right balance for a system to be generic enough so it can handle pretty much everything but specific and pragmatic enough to add value to your customers, with only a short development time to market. To me, the answer lies in the **close collaboration of tech with all other areas of your business** to make sure that the platform and the product are being built around the needs of your customers.

In the Captain Train/Trainline world this meant initially allowing connections for several hundred railway operators. But also, thinking ahead, we decided to add the facility of other modes of transport, in this case buses. By building in this sort of flexibility from the outset, we were able to add this without any significant disruption. However, retrofitting such an expansion, if your initial platform is too narrow, will be incredibly difficult and costly.

While the poor quality of a supplier's data input makes your added value even more obvious, the caveat is that poor flexibility and reliability can also become a major barrier to scaling for you. A long outage of data supply could become a major incident for you.

Therefore, my strong advice is to negotiate **Service Level Agreements (SLAs)** with your suppliers to ensure a smoother ride of data flow to the back-end side while you scale.

Front-End

The front-end is the home of the user experience (UX). Each front-end partition has its unique set of functionalities. Some are customer facing through desktop or mobile, but others are not directly end-customer facing, such as an Application Programming Interface (API) or internal services such as for your CS teams. Consider, also, your suppliers: why not offer a great front-end to your partners in the industry? Your application may give them access to metadata that provides them with information on their own services that they wouldn't be able to extract themselves. Ideally, you add so much value in the processing of their data from back- to front-end that these suppliers might become your customers also. This then creates an excellent strategic partnership, with interdependencies that will help your commercial discussions.

If possible, don't give in to the temptation to build out separate platforms for parts of the business to meet specific needs, especially around B2B. That is not only incredibly distracting and a waste of energy, but also completely unnecessary, if you have built out your platform in the right way. What you need to have is a product **flexible enough to account for multiple user flows**. As long as customers' data flows through your system and you achieve great economies of scale from it, you don't care whether your customers are consuming your product via your branded version or via a solution you have made available to third parties. This can even become your USP: with one platform, the external solution will always be to the same high-quality level that you guarantee to offer in your own branded channels. A competitor hosting two separate platforms will always give less attention to their partner platform and issues might only be noticed through them rather than directly. Based on this amazing quality and flexibility of your platform, you can now adapt it to meet all kinds of external customers' requirements in your front-end, giving them different **functionalities and integration depths to choose from**.

Make available to them a flexible API solution, which allows them to consume your data through different **integration depths**. As illustrated below, a new entrant might be simply forwarding its customers to your website to test traction, whereas a mature player with a strong brand is more likely to choose from a list of complementary functionalities to ensure its customers stay within their brand experience throughout their customer journey.

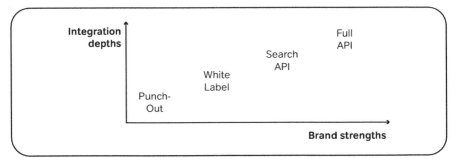

Fig 14: *Integration Depth – Maturity Diagram*

In the early-scaler chapter, I tried to raise awareness of the need to create your platform in a way that ensures reliability and flexibility. There is no way to scale successfully when your features break regularly, or you hit capacity bottlenecks. Choose an infrastructure and technologies that are proven to be reliably scalable. If there is an existing tool on the market that can do the trick, don't reinvent the wheel. Your framework and features such as geo-localising are not the parts in which to be an on-the-edge pioneer. It might be popular amongst some engineers, but it doesn't add value and it increases your inhouse maintenance effort. But there are **3 more key things a great platform needs**, to be scalable:

1. **Ensure security at all times**. You can't scale a product that customers don't trust. If you leak their credit card information, you are dead. Along with reliability and flexibility, any high quality, innovative product must have security as the cornerstone of their platform.

2. **Build <u>one</u> platform per product** only. For most scale-ups that means having precisely one platform only. Acquisitions and other legacy IT can lead to having several products with different platforms for different markets or different target groups. If this can be merged into one experience, bring it together wherever you can. The only thing that is more painful than a rebranding is a re-platforming, especially when you're in the middle of hyper growth. I'm speaking from experience. Maintaining more than one platform makes it a nightmare to scale, as it multiplies your required hosting and maintenance effort. At a certain point it becomes unmanageable, and you will inevitably decide to bring it all onto one platform eventually.

    Amalgamation also means that you **minimise the number of coding languages** within each area of your platform. In the front-end you might not be able to achieve this across all apps and the web, but in the back-end you should ensure that you operate with one language only. Also, don't go for trendy new languages that have not yet proven to scale. The risk is simply too high that what is trendy today could fall out of fashion tomorrow, leaving you in a place where you can't hire enough engineers just at the point when you need to grow.

3. **Oversee your IT recruitment strategy**. While you grow your platform with its connections and services, you need to continue to maintain and test everything frequently. It is not enough to work on shiny new features only. And therefore, you shouldn't just hire developers, or it will be them ending up providing (expensive) support to keep the system running, which will distract them from developing your platform and product.

   Therefore, after hiring front- and back-end and more flexible full-stack developers, consider hiring DevOps engineers for the following responsibilities: network, server and other hardware maintenance, infrastructure, and security.

Create a world-class product

Your product is your business card. It's key to customers, investors and, frankly, everybody will have a view on it. So, you need to make sure that it is a central part of the story you sell.

But what distinguishes an excellent product from merely a good one, other than the fact that it solves a specific customer need? Here are the **top-3-things that stand out in a world-class product**:

1. **User experience and a great design**. To me what this implies firstly is that even if you haven't read the user manual, your intuition is enough to guide you to where you need to get to. As a user, when I expect to confirm my purchase by clicking on the top right of the screen, and it's there as I hoped, then to me this feels like a good product – as if the creator was in my shoes. Secondly, it manages to reduce complexity of something complicated. Nobody needs a superficial super-app. Focus on solving the one thing you're best at all the way through. In the world in which I operated, train and bus tickets could be bought from different companies with different tariffs. The key was to think like the customer and ask ourselves how they can get from A to B in the quickest and cheapest way. We then ensured we showed them those options clearly, allowing them to book in an instant.

2. **Allow issues to be solved within the product**. As a user, I don't want to stick around in the product for longer than necessary, even if a complication arises. I want to be able to manage changes or cancelations directly through the product without having to contact someone or having to search for the answer. If you make your customers' lives easy in this way in complicated situations, they will remember this and will keep coming back.

3. **Same flow and key functionalities across all channels**. When I start a search on your app on my phone, I may want to switch to complete a transaction on your website. To do so, there needs to be all the same logic and key features in place across all channels. Don't be dogmatic though: don't be slowed down by waiting to ship features onto all channels where they don't add value from a user perspective. For example, depending on your product, you might not need to display notifications on your web version, whereas it's probably a must-have in your apps.

If you feel that you have implemented all of the above already, do not congratulate yourself just yet. The real challenge is still ahead, that of sustaining that level of excellence while growing fast and adapting to new target groups. For example, when you add a new country, translating your sites and apps into another language might be a no-brainer, but to harmonise some functionalities for all your target groups in one product will become difficult. Imagine that your home country lies in Europe, with customers being used to flying airlines that have four different booking classes, all of which you display in your product. You now want to expand your business into Qatar, where the national carrier only offers two booking classes. Would you still show all four of them? You will need to find your right middle way that works best for all customers, without having to change the core flow of the product.

Scaling your product

Your target groups will also change over time. In the beginning, your audience might be clearly ring-fenced as young, informed, tech-savvy and urban. To prove that you're able to take on the world, you must leave your comfort zone. While in a start-up the product is there to please a niche, say early adopters in one city. A scale-up needs to create a product or service which can satisfy the needs of as many customers as possible in a wide range of market sectors. That change is what should be your main concern from hereon in, and that is the part that most companies struggle with. Consequently, the second half of this chapter will look at **the things you should start doing to scale your product**.

1. **Start from the end**

   You need to be precise about what issue you want your product to solve. When you are building a ship to make the voyage to New York you can add an extra motor to help it to go faster, and you can also paint it blue, if that is your favourite colour. But adding wings won't make it a plane. You can add features, but only those which add value to the original structure. You decided that you are going by ship and therefore you arrive by ship at your final destination. Perhaps a better version of the ship you once started with, but it's still a ship.

2. **Adopt the right mindset and listen to your customers**

   Just like marketing or every other service function of your business, your product should serve one cause only: your customers' needs. You're not creating it for yourself, and neither your peers nor family and friends should decide whether it is what's needed. It is your customers alone that can make this judgment call. That doesn't mean that you shouldn't set the highest quality standards in what you build. But it does mean that **you should never assume** that what you consider great is what the customer actually requires. And the only way to **find the perfect product-market fit** is to go out there and test it. Let your clients actively engage with your product as early as possible so that they can provide you with constant feedback. So, I recommend that you do not wait until you have a quasi-final version but launch a Minimum Viable Product (MVP) as early as you can. Such a first version requires less time and fewer people to develop it, and you will get invaluable feedback from the market early in the game so that you can make modifications. Repeat this iteration until the product fits the market needs and do this before you then build out more features on that solid foundation. Ideally, as a start-up you will have new releases and refinements being added every other day, unlike large corporates with, say, just two a year, so you can be quick to react if necessary. That cycle-time agility will make all the difference while you scale and grow.

   Also, encourage your co-workers to use the product every day and in every possible situation, to unearth potential bugs and compare their experiences with your benchmarks. I know a couple of CEOs who check instantly what their competitors are doing, with every new idea that comes up. These reality checks are essential for the spirit and the level of excellence of the whole team, not just for the product-focused members. Obviously, when you put your heart into a product and you start identifying with it, it's not always easy not to take feedback personally. But you need to let go of your ego and be willing to reinvent yourself constantly.

While the company grows, it becomes more complicated to **stay in contact with customers** directly and on a regular basis. Here are a few things that I have seen work beautifully to stay on course as closely as possible.

- **Use your Customer Service team**. They are on the front line with your customers. Use and structure the feedback they get, trying to identify patterns. The mutual link between the CS team and the product is crucial. Make sure that there is dedicated engineering power to fix large, reoccurring issues in a way that ensures customers can increasingly self-serve themselves with the product.

- **Start online communities**, where users can give feedback, or opinions on new features. Have them participate in beta tests and occasionally organise events to help these communities feel that their feedback is being taken seriously, and that they are an integral part of the product journey.

- **Install a customer board**, where you have a fixed group of representatives of customers sitting together with the CEO and members of your product team on a regular basis to talk about their observations regarding your product. The fact that it's always the same group of people helps to compare the quality and performance of the product over time and to spot change.

- **Use focus groups** to test new features, especially before you enter new markets. Summarise the learnings, record the sessions and include as many colleagues as possible. Play this back to the whole team in the all-hands meetings. Every single person in your business should be aware of the biggest product challenges and should feel passionate about solving your customers' issues.

3. **Focus on impact**

   While I spoke about the importance of ensuring an equal quality level across all channels, the **mobile-website experience** is often neglected. It is, however, your entry gate and business card, as it is where most of your customers will land once you have turned on your marketing machine. Therefore, I strongly recommend making it your priority in both responsiveness and feature parity.

   Increase your **web-to-app** efforts (not only through marketing), by suggesting the app download as a key stage in the check-out flow and via push notifications. You want your satisfied customers to use your product as much as possible and therefore drive them to download your app, which will increase your retention rate.

Improve your Funnel. Improve your Funnel. Improve your Funnel.

While the previous scaling points are important, here is one that is essential to successful scaling your product, once that is, you have found your product-market fit. Start by defining what your North Star is. What is that one thing you want your customers ultimately to do at the bottom of the funnel? For e-commerce businesses, like the one illustrated below, this is straightforward: it is purchasing a product or service. For other digital businesses like streaming services the metric might read slightly differently and go from registering and downloading the app to ultimately buying a subscription. And yet, the objective remains the same: ensuring that you convert as many customers as possible from the top to the bottom of your funnel.

During the time that the funnel isn't optimised, there is no point in wasting marketing euros to generate demand. Your expensively acquired visitors would just disappear in the midst of the funnel instead of bringing in additional revenues. And yet, I've hardly ever seen teams being totally motivated in putting all their energies into fixing a funnel. That's a shame, because what could be sexier than helping your customers to get to your North Star? Still not convinced? OK, let me give it another shot: engineers love maths and visualisation, so maybe that's how I can get you.

In our case, the North Star objective was to get the customer to book a ticket and pay for it. The conversion rate = North Star/Total Visitors, which in the example below would lead to = 50/1000 = 5%. In words: only five percent of your visitors complete the check-out process to purchase through your platform.

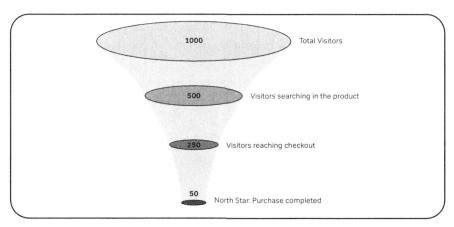

Fig 15: *Funnel of a digital product*

Now, you might wonder whether 5% is a good number for a conversion rate. It obviously depends on the industry and the product. But as a guiding reference, the figure ideally shouldn't be less than 2.5%, with champions achieving 10% and higher. The 5% in our example might not be bad in this instance, but it's not important where you stand today. What you want to prove is that you can increase it significantly, quickly and continuously. This is not a one-time exercise but should be the prevailing one throughout your scaling.

I'm not done trying to convince you to invest in the quality of your funnel process. Yes, it's meticulous work, with small, incremental, often almost invisible changes in the product being less exciting than adding a new feature – I get that. But the truth is that even the tiniest funnel change might have a hundred times more impact on your revenues than the biggest blinking new feature!

I hope my plea has hit home and that you're ready to get to work now. Before you start, make sure that you can track the correct data the whole way through the process, or you will be groping in the dark, wasting your time guessing. By doing so, we were able to pinpoint which part of the funnel was broken and then test our way towards finding the devil in the detail. By fixing this blockage in the funnel through a seemingly minor change, we were able to **double our conversion rates**. You will now have understood that there are no magic screws to turn, but still, there are **3 things I've seen that can have a huge impact on your funnel**:

1. **Loading Speed:** This is critical, with that of your site and app needing to be under 1 second. Amazon and Google have produced statistics on that: with every second you add, you can see a drop of a two-digit percentage of potential customers who might never come back.

2. **Readability:** Make sure that your sites are mobile friendly and fully responsive, especially now that most people will entirely use your product on their mobile devices. This is no longer optional but essential. A non-responsive site not only creates an unprofessional impression and may even be perceived to be a fake site, but also makes the purchasing journey difficult if not impossible. Remarkably, in spite of such high smartphone usage, this basic error still happens far too often!

3. **A purchase button:** This may sound crazy, but there are still sites out there with no obvious button to buy on them, or if there is one it is impossible to find. I have regularly had to abandon attempts to purchase things because I simply didn't see where I could do so. I worked for one company that rightly insisted: "When there's no booking button, add one or get rid of the site", and that goes too for every single sub site you create. And the location of the button is just as important. A-B-

testing can help you to best place it. These are the things that will re-write your conversion story.

A product star is hard to find

Just like everybody outside the company, inside your business, your colleagues will all have an opinion on your product. However, that is not a good reason to democratise product-related decisions. You need to put your customers first; deliver fast and to the highest quality, and you simply can't involve the whole team just because everybody has an opinion on the product. Leave it to the specialists to decide. More important for company-wide involvement is to lay out the roadmap in a proactive transparent manner to keep everybody burning for your product and its development.

Unfortunately, excellent product people are hard to find, for a couple of reasons. Firstly, this is a relatively new position which is still not taught at universities. However, change is coming, with initiatives like 'Maria Schools' in France that specialise in this niche to train more great product people. Secondly, there is a difference between a product manager and a UX designer, who is the person in charge of the visual appearance of the product. This is another group of superstars you need, who unfortunately are no easier to find.

Who is this rare, mystical product person we are desperately searching for everywhere? Here is the set of qualities that I looked for in recruiting an outstanding product person:

- People person with good listening skills
- Project manager with good leadership and negotiation skills
- Customer obsessed
- Visual visionary
- Data driven and commercial thinking
- Credibility with the engineers

As explained in the organisation chapter, to scale a company successfully, your product must remain at the heart of your business across all teams. This will also determine the effectiveness of the product people, who lead without hierarchical power. Therefore, should even the CEO be close to the product and have a vision and strategy? He should not get in the way operationally but have a vision, set the tone, and emphasise the importance of the product through his words and actions.

What makes the product people's life hard enough is that most tech driven businesses struggle with committing to **resources and deadlines** – to the point that it's culturally considered an insult to ask an engineer how long they would need to finish a project. You need to explain that it's not an attempt to compromise quality or question productivity, it's simply essential that no team can (continue to) work in silos. The business needs to operate as one and has dependencies between deliverables throughout the different teams. How can a new feature be promoted, and a communication plan defined, when there is absolutely no transparency on when it will be delivered? Furthermore, new code sometimes can be bad code and might produce issues that you would want to eradicate before marketing it in production. Bake that buffer into your planning and bring the tech and product team on that journey with you, or your growth will come to an end before you can even take off.

Most tech people I meet are super smart, human and sometimes rather sensitive souls who simply want to understand the bigger picture. Therefore, don't just impose a deadline, but provide more information and ask them to suggest one from their side. That is a great starting point for a negotiation, likely to make it a more realistic one through that joint commitment. The other thing is to align the objective's output better: tech wants to build the perfect experience and marketing wants to acquire as many customers as possible. These objectives do not stand in opposition to each other but need better communication on the common goal: both want to win a market or a target group and will only succeed together. In addition, alignment is motivating and provides more freedom to the individual deliverables of the squad-members. All these measurements combined will put the product back to the centre of everybody's attention, right where you need it.

Use your data to anticipate the future

Data is a great way to track your growth and follow how you solve the issues encountered by your customers. However, when I hear, "Be data driven", I say: be careful. Let me explain myself, using an impressive story from WW II, where the US Navy lost many aircraft and was looking into options to improve the planes to prevent more losses. What they did was to analyse where on the fuselage the planes had suffered the most damage. They looked at the planes that had been hit but had been able to return to base. They saw that most bullets had created holes around the wingtips and suggested to start with their reinforcement. A statistician named Abraham Wald disagreed, arguing that the Navy should reinforce the mid-body of the planes instead, because they were only looking at the planes that had made it back to base. Those which had disappeared had clearly been severely hit somewhere else and were impossible to examine. The Navy simply wasn't looking at a complete data set. And that's precisely why you should be careful looking at data to anticipate the future. It might not always hold the full set of information that you need to base your decision on. To quote Henry Ford, "If I had asked people what they wanted, they would have said faster horses", and the automobile would never have been invented. But to avoid any misunderstandings, data is indeed crucial to track progress and spot current issues on how to improve product, marketing or CS.

The real value comes with the data your customers bring into your world over time and your ability to use it to develop the future. Pending customer protection regulations, you have information on your customers' behaviour that you can use for marketing purposes, to better understand the industry and anticipate the future. A prerequisite to processing your data is to **implement a proper and scalable monitoring** infrastructure. The earlier you start, the more reference data you will have available to learn from. To extract the most from your data, hiring a data analyst will help you to undertake more profound analysis and get a sharper insight on important topics like funnel optimisation, conversion rate analysis or numerous marketing topics that we will speak about in the next chapter.

So, what are the areas where your business can profit from data and will once more increase your chances of winning a good round of tech bingo? Artificial intelligence, big data, and machine learning. They all have one thing in common: your machinery becomes more powerful from within, learning from your own data. When you play your cards right, it's an exponential upward spiral, creating greater value with every additional incoming data set. That's precisely where your scale-up process will catch your potential investors' curiosity.

I have always found these buzzwords a little intangible and had trouble imagining usage cases until I got involved in them myself. Here are a couple of examples from Trainline to illustrate what I'm talking about. The first one is on **crowdsourcing**, a thing we called 'BusyBot'. It's a crowd alert that uses the community to report how busy your part of the train is, to direct fellow passengers to less crowded areas. Every passenger who was about to board the train could now move to another carriage or even the next train. This kind of real-time feature solves an everyday issue and will involve your customer-community with your app even more.

The second example is one of **Artificial Intelligence (AI)**, using big data, something that we called 'Price Prediction'. This was about understanding the yield management systems in the transportation industry. We are all familiar with that situation when your ticket becomes more expensive the closer you get to the actual departure date, but then suddenly it becomes cheaper again to achieve the highest possible passenger load factor, and you are annoyed because you missed that sweet-spot moment. With a large portion of the market and millions of customers on our platform, we were able to learn how this works and to forecast how prices would develop. When we made this available to our customers and helped them to save money, we added a level of value that even the railway companies were not able or did not want to provide to their customers themselves. As a result, our customers became even more loyal to us.

But data can do something even bigger: it can **try to anticipate the future**. And when you want to be top-notch and a thought leader, you need to be on the verge of every new development, ideally ahead of the competition. I remember that Captain Train was one of the first transport companies worldwide to release an Apple Watch app, which got us into Apple's official launch communication. The same happened when Amazon Web Services (AWS) used Trainline as a usage case at their annual conference. That is the kind of endorsement you would want, to be taken more seriously by customers and potential investors.

However, be mindful of where you invest your resources. Data scientists and a good research and development team can help you to bid on the right trends and detect behavioural changes with your customers, but all this remains at best, a bet. And although I'm not Nostradamus, let me close this chapter with a short personal vision on the tech and product future: everything around sustainability is definitely going to be a winner. The only caveat is that we haven't yet decided what energy type we are going to use as fuel; my money is on hydrogen. I would also assume that blockchain, a harmonisation of payment methods and virtual reality will develop further in the future. Whereas trends around intelligent voice assistants have only seen a part of the success they have been forecasted to achieve. Personally, I haven't spoken to Alexa in over a year.

Top 3 Takeaways

1. Build one flexible, reliable and secure platform

2. Start your product thinking from the end and improve your funnel

3. Use your data to test, scale and anticipate the future in the best possible way

CHAPTER 7

The One-Billion-Euro-Story

I think it has become clear that my position stands in opposition to some of the tech founders. I believe that having a great product alone is not enough to achieve a successful exit. We agree that your company would be worth nothing without your product. However, unless you start spreading the news in an organised, professional way, it will remain a niche product and your business will be priced accordingly, if you even make it to an exit at all. Therefore, my piece of advice in this chapter is to follow the principle: do good and talk about it. We live in a world where **storytelling** has become so essential that your story counts as much as the product itself, with social media having hugely increased this phenomenon. Get your story right, let the world know how amazing your product is and create a hype around yourselves so that others tell your story for you. That's when you achieve great scaling effects.

Developing your story is not an easy task, but one that guides you to sharpen your mind on what to focus on internally and how you want the external world to perceive your identity. What is it that makes you distinct and that helps you to connect on a more emotional level with your potential target groups?

Looking at some other **brands** is a good starting point to get an indication of possible directions. What is the first association that comes to mind when you look at the following logos? Isn't it amazing that I don't even have to add colour or their brand names, and you still know which companies they represent?! And I'm certain that they even evoke an emotion in you, linked to a personal experience that you have had with their products and services. That's how strong they are. And I am also sure that you have confidence enough to leave your credit card data with them, which is the ultimate sign of trust. They have managed to step out of their niche to create a universal brand, by not limiting themselves to one market, target group or language.

So, how can you become such a recognised leading brand? You obviously need to think big, across geographies and about potential future target groups. However, you might be surprised to hear that it all starts by being brief and crisp. People won't remember more than a few key things about your business. Therefore, developing your clear, core messages is the most important task to start with. Feed into your internal experts and include specialised agencies to come up with a first suggestion. Then have it challenged by the leadership team before you test it in focus groups with potential target groups. It's a lengthy process that will repeat itself several times, until you begin to feel comfortable. That's why I would not present your brand story to the full team before you haven't decided on a final version, or the discussions will be endless. Also, test it with your other stakeholders to see how they react. Bring all the information together and adapt your story until you feel that you have one aligned version to go public with. You need to feel comfortable with your messages, as you will be expected to deliver against them. And only when you believe in your story will you be able to authentically and credibly shout about it from the rooftops.

But **branding** is more than storytelling – it's a real science. Based on the above, your branding experts will find a slogan and visualise your corporate design and identity. For example, Captain Train was known for being humanly relatable, creatively funny and freshly modern, which we represented with our unique tone of voice, the way we told jokes in between the lines, and cartooning our brand visuals. Being clear on your identity will now allow you to feed into all the other communication and marketing channels that you should use to scale-up your business.

Books about marketing are often written in a very academic way, from an organisational perspective, keeping communication and branding entirely separated and distinguishing between on- and offline marketing. For me all are part of marketing and anyway, this chapter is not about marketing for the sake of doing marketing, but how it can be used in the most impactful way to successfully scale and grow the business. I will describe the mechanisms of all the key channels and tools in relation to the timeline of a scale-up as it grows and acquires more money to spend.

However, before we continue, I have a few general heads-up for you, to get things right from the beginning. Just like on the product, absolutely everybody will have an opinion on your marketing activities, particularly as they become more visible. I could count to three until people called me after we had launched a TV commercial or had put posters up at metro stations. But, here as well, it's not important what your family or friends think – you must care exclusively about your target groups' reaction. That's why it's so important to be in close contact with your customers to be able to gauge their opinion at every turn.

What makes your life more complicated is the fact that good marketing people are rare, and while you will receive thousands of job applications, unfortunately, only a handful will be good enough for you. Don't be blinded by their storytelling – instead, test their suitability, especially around digital paid marketing. Hiring the wrong person in one of these areas can throw you back by a year or more, time and money you can't waste at this stage. This is what happened to us early in the game, before we found some of Europe's finest, who today are among the most chased individuals in the European scale-up ecosystem.

In summary, marketing, communication and branding aims to achieve two different objectives:

- **Consumer-facing: acquire and engage with new customers/generate demand.** Use all relevant media to increase visibility, develop awareness of products and services, encourage the purchase and then drive retention.
- **Corporate-facing: increase the value of the company.** Heighten the value of the brand; raise your profile and improve your image to attract investors, new employees and lobby regulatory bodies and governments.

The overall task of marketing is to get customers and potential investors interested in trying your product and services. After you have found your product-market-fit and have fixed your funnel, following the advice in the previous chapter, the assumption is that once they use the perfect product you've created, it will generate revenues. And, having more customers on your platform that spend money with you will increase the value of the company. But by targeting investors separately, your company value can grow exponentially even higher than your revenues. Therefore, it's important to be clear on whether your campaign is aimed at the consumer or at corporate target groups. If you attempt to mix them up randomly in the same campaign, you risk reaching neither.

In this chapter, I am going to focus on the consumer, as demand generation is the most important element to grow at this point. I will come back to the corporate point in greater detail when we speak about creating traction closer to the exit in the final chapter. At this stage, only a selection of the channels I describe can be adopted for corporate communication as well, especially those around PR. For example, select only those parts of your story that will be interesting to investors, feed the tools with the right content and highlight what adds to your profile. Even though this becomes more relevant once you are preparing for an exit, keep in mind that it can't be built overnight. I therefore recommend starting with a light touch as early as possible and then ramp it up when you're close to the finish line. An example from the Trainline world would be to communicate a new route being made available in the product. This can work as two different stories. Consumer-facing, you can promote a new market, new products, and new services becoming available. For your corporate profile though, it would be more interesting for investors to learn that your platform powers X connections covering Y% of the relevant market now.

But for now, all eyes should be on the hottest prize, that of bringing the maximum number of new customers onto your platform. By default, I'm here referring to end-customers (B2C) but the following can easily be applied to business customers (B2B) or combinations (B2B2C) as well. Before we start generating additional demand, it is vital to double-check that you have found the ideal product-market fit and that the funnel is ready to convert new incoming customers all the way to the bottom so that the product is adapted for the pond we are now trying to fish in. Again, there is no point in bringing new customers to the top of the funnel when they find themselves confronted by a product that doesn't fit their needs or just doesn't let them purchase from you.

And it's also in the platform logic where we find the answer to the question: "How do we know how many new customers we ought to acquire in what area?" As many as possible obviously, but more precisely, what you want to arrive at is a supply-demand-equilibrium. In other words, acquire new customers where you have available supply. A surplus of either is a waste of resources and capacities. For example, for Booking.com it's acquiring new customers for the hotels in Spain they have just added, and for Spotify it is identifying people wanting to listen to the new album by Adele. Finding this optimum point is the objective for pretty much any marketplace.

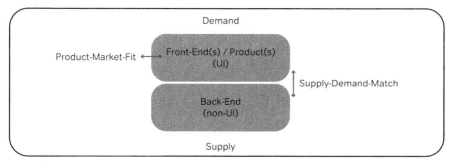

Fig 16: *Product-Market-Fit & Supply-Demand-Match on a digital platform*

Customer acquisition should be everybody's obsession from day one and not only for the tech, product and marketing teams. Everything that is done in the company should be around how to bring in and engage with the customer. To achieve that, you have two categories of marketing channels available to you:

- **Organic** (no marginal cost per new customer)
- **Paid** (incurs a cost for every new customer)

As a start-up you take off by using whatever free channel you can find. Once you successively manage to get your hands on more money to scale, buy yourself more marketing power and be more selective with your tools. In that line of thinking, I am going to present to you the main channels, from totally free to super expensive, and their impact to achieve your objective to generate as much demand as possible. However, you don't need to be great at them all. You need to find your own way and discover what works best for your product and your target groups. If you manage to champion one or two of the channels below, it can carry you far. A lot of the big players out there, like Airbnb and Booking.com owe their success (besides having a great product) to becoming world champions in just a couple of the following acquisition channels.

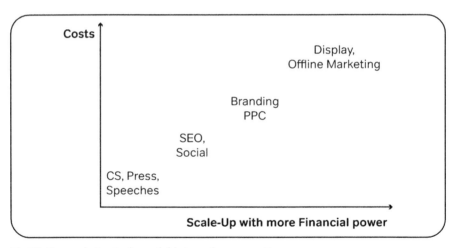

Fig 17: *Key marketing tools available to scale-ups over time*

Organic Channels

The story you have written about yourself and the image you have decided to create serve now as a starting point to use in your marketing activities to spread the news. As promised, we are starting with the organic channels that allow growing from within with no external costs involved. The only costs that apply here are those linked to your internal headcount working on these channels and any relevant software fees.

Some of these tools might even come as a surprise to you, or have you considered all the following to be part of your marketing portfolio?

- Your **Customer Service (CS)** can become a key marketing USP and a great brand ambassador, especially in the beginning. Treating your customers in a human, individual manner will gain you a reputation which can increase your word-of-mouth propaganda.

  In Europe, customers use as many as between 3 and 4 channels on average to contact customer service. Each new channel adds a challenge and complexity. For example, if customer service can be accessed via social media, someone needs to be checking this constantly to protect your brand reputation. Then add more relevant FAQs and highlight self-service to avoid people having to contact you on simple matters. And while you should keep it that way for as long as possible, over time, to be able to scale, you will need to add a lower quality second level of support for the more basic questions. That will change your tone to parts of your customer base, and your customer service USP inevitably slowly becomes weaker.

- Create and use **your blog** to communicate corporate news and product developments to bond with your customers and potential investors. Bring them on the journey with you and increase your number of loyal visitors. Also use it to position yourself as a thought leader, as an expert reference point in your sector. Whatever you use your blog for, make sure that it is optimised for SEO, and I suggest making it as public as possible, not an exclusive closed-shop solution. On top of this, your blog content can be reused on social media or for Customer Relationship Management (CRM) purposes. It is important to align your messaging throughout all these channels. This is then the first step to Public Relations (PR) and a start to defining your tone of voice.

- **Building and engaging with your community** through social networks has become a powerful tool to increase trust and awareness of your brand. More and more people will check on your number of followers before purchasing. Make them feel part of your story and your network and do everything you can to encourage them to talk about you. Just like on your blog you can speak about upcoming features, take feedback on issues, as well as making them share their thoughts and requests about your product. Just be mindful that this needs proper resource staffing – it can quickly develop its own dynamic that risks escalating out of control if not properly monitored and managed.

- Another way to win trust with potential new customers is using **customer reviews** (Tripadvisor, Google reviews etc.). These are quasi free and a powerful tool to increase confidence in your brand and raise the likelihood that potential customers will click on your snippets (SEO or PPC links to your product). This can be extended to paid versions like Trustpilot and others, if you see that this is a tool that works for you.

- Take up **speaker opportunities** at relevant events that you are invited to. You might even be able to add your logo, slogan or a short description of yourselves on the event's website or flyer. A great speech can gain you empathy as well as credibility and get people to start talking about you. It also allows you to test yourself and your speaker qualities. The more traction you get, the more comfortable you should feel to stand on large stages.

- One of the key instruments in this section is one that I briefly touched upon in the early scaler chapter: **SEO** – **S**earch **E**ngine **O**ptimisation. In a nutshell, it is what pops up in the Search Engine Result Page (SERP) after the ads when searching for a keyword. Your objective is to rank at least in the top 3 (=70% of clicks). And the new grail of SEO is the so-called 'Position 0', which is the featured snippet block at the top of the SERP that displays whole written answers to your keyword search. SEO will in large part decide how successfully and at what acquisition cost ratio you will scale. The good news is, we are still in the organic channel section, and the costs associated with SEO consist exclusively of the people working on it. And while SEO is one of the tools that is equally important for start- and scale-ups, the difference lies in the manpower you dedicate to it while you grow. Please hear my recommendation loud and clear: It takes time to be ranked high and you cannot start too early to put a significant amount of resource into the two different aspects to SEO:

    i. **The content part:** This needs to be unique and rich, embedded with images and videos. It should include relevant keywords and links to other pages in your world, but any article should still be readable. Google will rank you higher over time when you constantly change, localise and add as much useful content as possible. Test your way through it and track keyword searches of your customers to understand what they are searching for. You can then create the content in the style that attracts them.

ii. **The technical part:** This improves the quality of your pages. Your search engine and your customers will reward quick loading times (especially including videos), safety (secure your website with https) as well as mobile responsiveness. Yet again, add the famous purchase button to *every* page.

- The last one of the organic channels that I want to mention deserves as much recognition. It's **PR, with a focus on press work in particular**. I have seen press having the most amazing impact from the beginning to the end of my scale-up experiences. I remember when I joined Captain Train, our PR work was hugely successful. And as it was pretty much the only thing we did on the marketing side, we could prove that any wins were coming purely from this PR effort. Also, on the corporate side, neither the M&A nor the IPO would have been possible without excellent press work. But besides proactively pitching your story, PR also has a reactive side to it, which can be key to avoiding disasters and serves as effective damage control. As I have experienced the power that PR can have when managed by the right people, allow me to elaborate a bit further:

  i. **The role of the PR person.** Their primary role is to broadcast a selected part of your story through press releases, press conferences and interviews, and ensure that these stories land at exactly the moment that coincides with your other marketing activities. It's also a form of relationship management. Externally, you need to build up a trusted journalist base that you can engage with and who respect confidential information. Internally, it's about building a spirit of teamwork and having experts feed in. Used correctly, PR is a great internal marketing tool as well, as it can make the teams proud when they read about their company in the press.

  ii. **Proper preparation and orchestration are vital.** At all times you need to be mindful about what content to communicate. You need a red-lined consistency in the messages taken from your story that everyone in the business follows, if asked. And remember, once a part of the story gets out, it can't be taken back. That's why you should be highly selective on what you communicate, especially regarding your numbers. Help by writing boiler plates with the key facts about your company and prepare briefings with FAQs which the spokesperson should learn by heart.

iii. **Have designated spokespeople.** These are the *only* people allowed to speak on behalf of the company publicly and be the face of the business to the market. This is usually the founder and/or CEO, but it can occasionally be experts, when properly briefed on specific topics. I strongly recommend having media training. This is a profession that must be learned. I have seen CEOs screwing up interviews in their early days, and yet coming back a year later rocking the show and enjoying themselves. It's worth the investment in yourself and for the company.

iv. **Work with a PR agency early on.** Start with a small one or even a freelancer and change to more specialised agencies over time, perhaps even per country and separate ones for consumer and corporate. You remain in charge, and it's for you to manage them and make sure that they tell your story effectively. Only you know whom you want to attract, so they can only help you on the execution.

Monitor your impact

You now have an overview of all the organic channels that you ideally already applied before you started scaling. Unfortunately, except for SEO, being entirely digital, all the above have one weakness in common: they are very poorly trackable to **measure their impact**. So how are you supposed to know if you are putting your money on the right horse? Well, there are attempts from the PR side to look at Monthly Unique Users (MUU) to measure its reach, but it doesn't necessarily give an indication on how many actually read your interview and how many readers try your product as a result.

Earlier, I spoke about the channels having to work hand in hand. PR and SEO are good examples of that. They should create content together. Journalists want news to sell their papers and need convincing to write about you. And they will never do you the favour to include any links in their articles. When you create some data-driven content however, journalists are more likely to link it, for example, to your new cool tool to calculate your carbon footprint, which then allows you to track success through backlinks.

On the branding side as well, brand trackers can help you to measure the development of your brand awareness. They ask whether your product comes to mind when thinking about your category or industry, and if potential customers would consider using your product. And even though a high two-digit percentage of brand awareness gives you an indication of becoming well known, it does not precisely tell you how many new customers you acquired from every additional euro spent. A caveat on branding from my personal experience: you can easily get blinded by your own surroundings. I remember that despite everybody knowing and loving Captain Train in Paris, I was super surprised that the brand was almost entirely unknown as soon as I left the city. In summary, there is just no proof on the precise impact of branding and PR – you just need to believe in its effectiveness, like I do.

Not being able to make the direct link between your initiatives and the impact they have on your demand generation might not be a drama in the beginning: you invest little, and you are far from reaching any ceiling in your identified target group. But this becomes a whole different story when you're trying to scale, spending significant amounts of money to tackle new target groups. You want your marketing spend to be as impactful as possible on your mission to scale and attract investors. And here's some good news – paid digital marketing is perfectly trackable. It's never grey, it's either black or white. And as it's so tangible, tracking its success is mostly analysing numbers. The only prerequisite is that you **implement the right tracking tools** to be able to monitor the results of your spending. As a positive side-effect, all the wannabe marketeers will calm down when you let the numbers speak for themselves. But heads-up, you cannot just endlessly throw money at it and expect it do the trick by itself. You will need to do your homework and conduct data-based market research to identify potential new target groups first. But where you can monitor closely everything you do, your learning curve will be greater with every additional euro you invest. You can also use paid channels to support less trackable branding. Use it to test messaging upfront, for example.

I said that you could calculate the success of your paid channels, so you rightly expect a formula and definitions at this point. Let me try to make it as tangible for you as a take-away as possible. It all comes back to the unit economics of a digital platform, to associate the costs that occur to acquire a new customer. Or in other words, **will it be profitable for the business to acquire this new customer?** And the answer is yes, if the revenues the new customer generates over time are higher than the costs to acquire them. Here is what you need, to be able to answer that question.

The Definitions:
- **Cost per Acquisition (CPA)** = The total cost of a campaign/number of new acquired customers through this campaign (not necessarily paying customers)
- **Customer Acquisition Cost (CAC)** = Expenses (marketing and sales)/number of new customers acquired (actual paying users)
- **Customer Lifetime Value (CLV)** = Total amount of money a customer is expected to spend in your business during their time using your product and services = (Annual revenue per customer * customer relationship in years)

The Formula:

> ### CAC < CLV and/or CPA < CLV
>
> - **Decrease your CPA and CAC**
>   - by increasing your organic growth ratio vs. paid
>   - by increasing your brand awareness and consideration
>
> - **Bring your CLV up** by increasing your retention rate

If you have absorbed the formula in this box, you have got to the bottom of the objective of marketing in your scale-up – you can continue to spend as long as your CLV is larger than your acquisition costs. I wish that somebody had explained this to me this clearly at times, as it would have saved me so much trouble, and I would have stopped investing in a few lost causes.

Paid Channels

The prospect of having found the perfect measurable tool to successful scaling, and ensuring you know exactly your upper spending limit, should make you super excited. Before we continue, a little reminder that scaling doesn't mean you must grow your spend in direct proportion to your revenue. You should still be looking for ways to spend marginally less for every additional customer. You want to prove that you can manage to scale through learning. To get there, as described above, you need to steadily bring down your average acquisition costs. That's why you have a huge interest in not exclusively using paid channels from here on in either. You need to develop further your organic channels, ramping them up so that they take a relatively high percentage in the demand generation portfolio. Every free customer is literally a gift on your way to achieving this objective. Increase your SEO effort to sustain a good ratio. To decrease your CPA, continue to spend on branding to create confidence. Your customers are more likely to click on a link of a brand they trust.

In theory, all this sounds straightforward. However, the execution can be a challenge at times. Let's go through the paid channels, and I'll explain one-by-one how you can master them.

- The first and most important representative in this category answers to many different names. At university you might have got to know it under Search Engine Marketing or -Advertising (SEM/SEA), and in the scale-up world it's often referred to as **Pay Per Click** or for short, **PPC**. No matter what you call it, this channel allows you to scale immediately because of its huge reach. What it does can be described in a nutshell as follows: you're throwing all your money at your search engine to ideally be ranked on top of every page in the ad section. But be mindful, costs can quickly explode. To give you an idea of the crazy amounts that are being spent: The Booking Group alone spends more than €3bn a year on this one tool to buy an important chunk of their growth.

But putting all your money in an envelope and sending it to Google is not going to do the trick. As a prerequisite, just like for SEO, you need to bring up your quality score, which rates your relevance and the quality of your ads. Get your tech and product teams involved to ship great ad copies and landing pages. It's also your business card and the first thing a new customer might see from you.

Then you need to determine your objectives. Depending on your KPIs and whether you want to increase sales or find new customers, you define your key words per market, language and customer group. At one point however, you will reach a ceiling and need to be reactive to always add new keywords. Other parties putting their money on the same keywords will make the price go up and your chances to appear at the top then decrease. That is why in highly competitive markets, some keywords can be extremely expensive. And there are more roadblocks: when you want to bid on another brand name, you will have to ask for their approval first. Everybody tries to exclude as many parties as possible, claiming that it's all part of their brand. A priority of the regulator is to avoid confusion and never mislead the end consumer on what company one is purchasing from. There are brands that imitate other brands, which is not fair play and will harm their own brand the most in the longer run. Whatever way you play it though, in the end, there will be only one winner: Google.

And whether you like it or not, you will have to play along to stand a chance. Try to understand how the system works and build close relationships with people from Google to make the best of the outrageous amounts you're paying them. For completeness, even though this is a European story, you might still want to work in the Chinese market, where Google is blocked. In China, you will need to work with Baidu, which follows a pretty similar concept and tools, but is obviously much more restricted.

What you need to do on your side over time is **develop an internal machine-learning algorithm** to increase your keyword efficiency. In the iterating process of finding ever new keywords, you learn from your own history on how to optimise your own results. In the beginning, due to a lack of capacity, you might use an agency or a freelancer to run this for you. Make sure that you're aligned on the objectives and the budget from the start. However, developing this algorithm inhouse and proving that you can scale from within has a huge value to scaling and to potential investors. It deserves a proper playbook and will increase your valuation.

What you want to prove to potential investors is that you could scale limitlessly. They want to be reassured that you can find a way to scale even faster when they come in and double or triple your marketing budget. And based on our formula, what this means is, provided CPA / CAC < CLV, you can continue bidding until the doctor comes.

- The next channel, **social media ads**, combines an organic channel with a paid service. The efficiency of this tool very much depends on your product. I have seen Facebook ads work on a highly specific trend or lifestyle brand. It helps best in creating brand awareness rather than converting into leads. Therefore, it might not be the ideal instrument to generate broader demand. If you want to try it out, start with less established services that don't charge you as much, but could have a similar effect.

- Another common channel is so-called **display ads**. The performance of this channel really depends on the industry. What might come to mind first is a big-brother-watching-style awful image popping up on a non-related website linked to an earlier search. But it can also be a sponsored blogpost at the bottom of an article, which often performs pretty well. I recommend using this channel mainly for retargeting campaigns, to avoid massive CPAs. And to not be perceived as annoying, try to apply it in a way that adds value for the customer. You could suggest a rental car after the booking of a hotel in a rural area for example. You will have to accept though that you don't have control over where it will be displayed.

- **The cooperation of influencers** has become popular. You pay someone to promote you. The idea is to give potential new customers the perception of an agnostic evaluation by an independent person. This can be especially helpful when you want to be seen as an opinion leader or have a new feature to promote.

To make a difference with this channel, you would need to get hold of the truly influential people, who are expensive and hard to get. Unlike journalists, who choose topics according to their audience's interest to inform them, with influencers it's pure business, often agreed through their management. The upside is that you have more control about the content and, as it's usually entirely digital, it can be monitored. You should see it as a complementary option to PR rather than a standalone tool. It's not touching the same target groups and serves your brand awareness rather than acquisition, unless you add a promocode and create an incentive.

- In the absence of sufficient inhouse resources, it does make sense to look into **partnership and sponsoring opportunities** to benefit from their experience and expertise. Check whether their brand expresses what you stand for. And only work with them if you feel that the cooperation will help you to achieve your objectives better and faster. Also make sure that you're properly being represented in their world and that success can be monitored. Putting your logo on an evening event is rather for big corporates, whereas, for example, a specific online discussion on your topic of expertise can be of help for your profile and to acquire new business customers.

- Another form of such a partnership is **affiliate marketing** where you pay other websites a commission for each customer that they forward to you. Start by identifying the top 10 affiliates that normally represent 90% of the market and make sure that you appear on their site and apps through banners or links. But heads-up, it's a lot of tech administration and contractual hassle. I therefore recommend going through networks if you want to cover multiple smaller affiliates. I've seen it be an efficient tool, especially if you find a commercially viable deal that creates a win-win for both parties. Then they too have an interest to nicely feature you.

- If you pay others to be your ambassadors, it's called a **referral programme**. It's an accelerator of your free word-of-mouth, by incentivising customers and colleagues to convince their friends and family to become customers or co-workers themselves. It's a mechanism that I have found can create a lot of positivity, as scale-uppers are usually passionate about their businesses and great multiplicators. The calculation on how much you can pay them should be based on your estimated CLV again. I have one big caveat: it's regularly subject to fraud.

- We spoke about being invited to events and using them as a stage for your cause and opinion. With more money, you can go a step further and **create events** yourself. Here, you can position your business completely freely, but you need to attract the right sector heavyweights to generate further traction. Try organising an awards evening by recognising individuals in the industry you're trying to be a part of. Make PR and social media cover it beautifully.

- And last but not least, there is **offline marketing**. Putting posters in public places can help branding and will impress your target groups, potential investors and attract new talent. And it will certainly get you some great pictures on social media and for you to use in your own publications. But coming in big can also create tension with industry partners. The biggest downside however is that it's not digital, and therefore not trackable. And printing QR or promo codes on it won't change the game.

Engagement and retention

We have now covered how you create demand, but we haven't spoken about **retaining and keeping your acquired customers engaged**. With high CLV being the key to succeed to scale sustainably, this is equally important. We want every acquired customer to purchase as many times as possible, or whatever else you have defined as your North Star at the funnel bottom.

Let's use an example to illustrate why this is so important:
- Your CAC to acquire a new customer is €4
- This customer books one ticket for €40
- You receive 10% commission = €4

In that case, your CAC would equal your CLV of €4, so you didn't make any profit with this one. Whereas, when the same customer comes back and makes another booking, our holy formula CAC < CLV is true again, and you're good. So, you need to always look at the retention rate and activate customers wherever you can.

You want your customers to engage with your product and transact more often. Start by **identifying the right cohorts** that you will look at on a regular basis and use a proper **CRM system**. By the way, CRM is free, and aims at sending the right message to the right segment of customers at the right time. I'm coming back to the example I outlined, that of the importance of encouraging your customers to download the app after their purchase from your website, to keep them in your system. Following on from the lessons in the previous chapter, if the product team have taken the necessary actions on their side, then the marketing team should now, for example, follow up by suggesting the app download in a confirmation email.

Once you have them use your app, you can display free ads through in-product marketing. Suggest upgrades and increase the Average Transaction Value (ATV) to bring up your CLV. The challenge, again, is keeping your customers engaged without being perceived as annoying spammers. Make sure that you suggest things they genuinely care about, and don't offer a client a once-in-a-lifetime trip to Rome, when Rome is their home city. Use what you know about the customer and add value in a non-intrusive way. For example, send app notifications to remind them of the opening of a new booking horizon to their favourite destination. The trick once again lies in automating the processes. From there on, it will become scalable and will make engagement and retention a powerful completion to acquisition.

TOP 3
Takeaways

1. Identify your USPs to build a clear story for your business and branding

2. Be clear on whether your communication is consumer- or corporate-facing

3. Continue to use all organic channels extensively and add paid channels to generate more demand while keeping your customers engaged

SECTION III

The Exit
Preparation

CHAPTER 8

All On Green is Not On Track

A fter we have made our way through the key areas of your company to set it up for scaling, we are now getting closer to the exit. Before you can start going out and subtly signal that you're ready, you must make sure that you internally have put in place monitoring tools that at this stage should show great results. But heads-up, I have seen cases where all KPIs were showing a green light, and yet they were not on track to success. They were simply not monitoring the right things to drive the impact on their strategic goals. As a result, despite all their KPIs looking good, they were running in the wrong direction. If you set your burglar alarm at the front door only and a thief enters through the back door, you won't wake up until it's too late.

Ideally, this gets fixed before you move into scale-up mode and definitely before you plan to exit. This chapter is all about making those fixes. This may seem stuff that you think is a bit dry: your KPIs, budgeting and your liquid means more generally. However, once brought to life, you will appreciate the value they bring to win your game. The two important things to begin with are:

- Start monitoring early so that you have reliable and comparable data sets over time.
- Be mindful of what you share with the external world. What is out there cannot be taken back.

Tracking the right KPIs

So, what are the right **Key Performance Indicators (KPIs)** for you to track progress against your exit plan? Try to look at it from the end backwards, putting yourself in the shoes of a potential investor or buyer. What would they look at and want to see proven in your business before they become interested, and what is the right set of KPIs to illustrate that? It's important here to not just look at one possible exit option. You want to have a plan B, in case things don't work out as hoped. But either way, monitoring what you consider interesting internally is simply not enough. Now you need to start trying to please the external world too.

Your specific set of KPIs are unique to your business and your industry. However, you will have many KPIs in common with many other scale-ups. That's why I thought it might help to share my **Top 15 KPI list** that I have looked at on different boards over the years. However, you would never present as many as 15 KPIs, but rather select 5 or 6 that add up to creating a rounded picture. Be careful that they don't stand in conflict with each other, but serve as appropriate indicators, tracking progress on your most important strategic goals. Although you should have a steady set of KPIs to be able to track your development over time, the closer you come to the finish line, the more financial ones will need to be added.

Let us consider the first three KPIs:

1. Top Line Sales
2. Take Rate
3. Revenue

Platform businesses often sell on behalf of a third party and so don't get to keep the entire sales they generate. For example, if you sell a hotel night for €100, you may receive 10% commission and take a fee of €1. So, your top-line sales through your channels will have been €100, with your take rate (fees and commissions) of 11% or 11€ of revenues in this case. What counts in the end is the amount of revenue you generate, because that is what your valuation will be based on.

There are different ways to look at revenues. Depending on the industry, some businesses look at Annual Receiving Revenues (ARR) or at Gross Merchandise Volume (GMV). But no matter the perspective, revenue is the ultimate KPI to look at and vital to track from the beginning to the end. However, be careful about how transparent you want to be. I would never show numbers until an investor has signed an NDA, and prefer to stick to percentage growth instead, and even that only if absolutely necessary.

4. Gross Margin
5. EBITDA

If you take the revenues and deduct your associated costs that have been incurred to generate these revenues, you arrive at your gross margin. And if you take all the revenues and deduct all the costs to the company, not just the ones that are directly linked to your revenue, you can calculate your gross result or **E**arnings **B**efore **I**nterest, **T**ax, **D**epreciation and **A**mortisation (EBITDA). This latter measurement is definitely not one to show early in the game, for several reasons:

- Other than in the context of your liquidity, your EBITDA is not something you frequently look at it while you scale.
- It's good to have a plan to get to a break-even, but as long as you still have money in the bank, your key concern should be to grow as much and fast as you can.
- Once you start generating a profit, your flattering valuation based on a multiple of your revenues might be switched to be based on your profits. Unless you are a mature company this will hardly ever move in your favour.

At this stage you want to show that your playbook allows you to achieve marginally more output from every additional euro invested. If you have managed to break even early in your scaling phase, and I was to be your investor, my question to you would be, why haven't you spent the money? It's a(n) (ad)venture, where you can only make it big when you're taking a reasonable amount of risk.

6. Cash-Burn-Rate
7. Runway

While the above is true, your top preoccupation should always be how long your cash in the bank is going to last. It's like in *Super Mario*, when you have lost your last life, it's always game over. Whilst I would never externally show my cash-burn-rate, to not come across as needy when you are trying to raise money, it is an important indicator for you to look at, at least once a month. It's a rate that looks at how much money you burn per month and, on that basis, how long you will be able to pay your salaries and other invoices. Let's say you have €1m left with the cashier and you burn €100k per month, then your runway would be 10 months until you are running out of liquid means.

8. New Customers (NC)
9. Monthly Active Users (MAU)

One, if not your main objective at all times, is to gain new customers. Therefore, make sure that one of your KPIs indicates your progress on achieving this objective. And the more active your clients are, the more value they have for your business. Finally, it can help to track both KPIs also per target group (B2C vs B2B) and per market, to be able to track change when it happens.

10. **Cost Per Acquisition/Customer Acquisition Costs (CPA/CAC)**
11. **Conversion Rate**
12. **Customer Lifetime Value (CLV)**
13. **Retention Rate**

I have spoken extensively about these four in the previous chapter. I hope what you have taken from that is that they should be all part of every internal presentation and it is crucial to track them throughout your journey. So, let me just briefly remind you that you want to see a downward trend in your CPA and CAC. This indicates an increasing ratio towards organic versus paid search. By contrast, your CLV ideally should show an upward trend, as should your retention rate. These performance indicators have the granularity you need, to be able to track whether your scaling efforts are bearing fruits.

14. Brand Awareness

As discussed, measuring the effect of branding is difficult, so when can you confidently say that you have won in a market? One approach is to define a percentage of brand awareness and track yourself against it. I have spoken about the downsides of this approach and therefore recommend to not use it as a standalone KPI, but rather to see it as an indicator of decreasing CPA. And low CPA, combined with great NC and MAU numbers is what you need to achieve to win a market, given that you have a great product-market fit and your funnel is optimised. Branding can help with that, despite being debatable what the precise impact will be.

15. Customer Service Response Time

Every business needs to keep track of its operational excellence. The bigger you get, the more operations you have, the more can break and the bigger the impact will be when it does. Therefore, you need to monitor your quality level closely, with alarm bells going off if it dips, so that you can react immediately. Every business is different, with operational activities spread across various parts of your company. That is why I use the customer service centre as a representative example here.

You need one KPI that shows how well and how effectively you treat your customers. One way to measure satisfaction is to ask your customers to rate your service level. The problem with this is that it is often unhappy customers who bother to rate your service. As a result, this doesn't give you a representative view of your overall quality. Therefore, what I found to be more meaningful was measuring the average response time: how long does it take the CS team to get back to each customer? This would be measured in relation to the number of incoming tickets. Looking at that as a trend over months or even years can be a good indicator as to whether your team is correctly staffed.

So far, all these KPIs have been more or less tangible. But how do you track **people-related progress**, other than how much they cost and your headcount? How do you measure their wellbeing, morale and potential flight risks? It's not easy and leaves room for interpretation, but it's an important area to measure correctly. From my own experience, just starting to think about how you can measure team satisfaction helps already, as it begins to focus you on this crucial topic. If you don't look at this, issues within your team not discovered early enough have the potential, in a worst-case scenario, to bring your business to a complete standstill.

Here are two ideas on how to implement people-KPIs that I have seen work:

- **Internal surveys:** Ask your team anonymously, on a quarterly basis, the same 10 questions. Then, compare the results and follow up on them in all-hands and within each team. Your survey should include a question on leadership and give you indicators on how well each team is doing and on how well your managers perform in their roles. Be aware that these kinds of exercises can be counterproductive if no actions are taken based on the feedback received.

- **Mood boards** on how individuals are doing: I sat down monthly with my C-team and the HR head to talk about our key performers and those identified as our highest potentials. How are they doing, have we heard anything that should alert us, when is the next promotion due, and who is speaking to them and when. Doing this rigorously and regularly, aiming to show proactively that you care, is going to reduce unexpected flight risk.

Every business is different, and so it is for you to choose the right KPIs from this list. But no matter what your enterprise is, if I were on your board, I would want to see, at the very least, your revenues, MAUs and your runway on a monthly basis. I would also make sure that you looked regularly at your gross margin, conversion rate, the CLV and your team satisfaction internally. As a reminder, your KPIs should reflect what you are focusing on and ought to provide a monitor as to whether you are on track to achieve your strategic goals. These can then be broken down into Objectives and Key Results (OKRs) to align and hold your teams accountable.

However, displaying naked KPIs without providing any perspective can be misleading. If you were to tell me that your revenues are €5M, I would be unable to say whether this is good or bad. Add context by showing growth percentages versus last year (Year on Year – YoY) and compare these to your planned budget. But even then, caution is advised. A small start-up might achieve four-digit growth numbers and applaud itself. But their starting base was small too. Therefore, it's important to appreciate that marginal growth inevitably becomes smaller over time. These are all things a person can only read into the numbers when you **provide as much context as possible** and not just a small clip. The following are two ways of presenting your KPIs in a manner that helps your audience to better make a judgment on your progress.

	Actual YTD	vs Budget	YoY	RAG
KPI 1: Revenues	+50%	+49%	100%	Green
KPI 2: MAU	+25%	+30%	+50%	Amber
KPI 3: CLV	+1%	+10%	+2%	Red

Here, you present your numbers in growth percentages: Year To Date (YTD – from the beginning of your financial year until today), YoY and add a "Red Amber Green (RAG)" traffic light system at the end to be able to highlight weak spots straightaway.

Another way to illustrate the same KPIs is by using graphs. Many people are visual in how they prefer to interpret things. And while the grid above requires a certain routine in reading numbers, the graph on the next page may prove to be easier to spot aspects such as dips and seasonality. As much as this may help internally to get to the bottom of a potential issue, you need to **flatten out major negative trends** that could indicate that something is broken, before presenting it to the external world. Your story should read as a steady curve up to the top right, supported by your numbers and graphs. Things break and dips can happen, but what you need to show is that you were able to react, to repair any damage and get things back up and running smoothly.

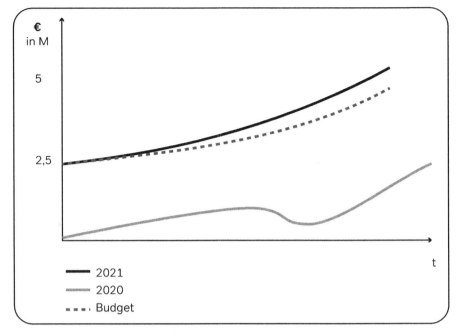

Fig 18: *Illustrating KPIs using graphs*

Budgeting and planning

So, what should your planning and budgeting process look like that determines realistic targets for your KPIs? The following illustration shows the four phases of a full year that should get your there. Involving parts of each team in this process will help the entire company to become much more sensitive to your KPIs. People will start considering these to be their numbers as well, and this is important. I have seen people in budgeting rounds where they didn't look as if they had ownership of their numbers, because they didn't feel that it was their plan too. This needs to be an iterative process that is not just top-down but allows for at least a couple of bottom-up loops as well. The people charged with delivering against each initiative must be given the chance to provide their input. It takes time, but it is a wise investment to ensure that everybody in charge has bought into the plan. At the stage where you get closer to the exit and the CFO is increasingly taking the lead, the mindset must change towards being more numbers-driven, and a professional way of managing the following process must happen. As a minimum, I expected every team member to know the company's top 5 KPI targets for the year as well as their team's and individual OKRs, and where we stood against all of them at any given point.

Let's now look at the four-stage planning, budgeting and reporting cycle, which can be summarised by this diagram:

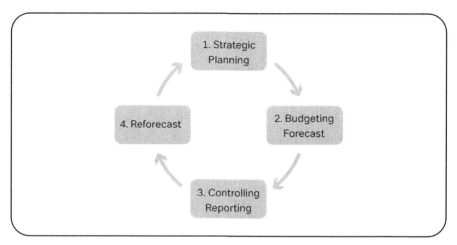

Fig 19: *Planning, budgeting and reporting cycle*

1. Starting from the top, planning and forecasting are exercises that are conducted once a year, ahead of the start of your new financial year. Combined, they shouldn't take longer than a couple of months. Even though this is extra time out of your agenda, it is important to get your planning right so that you're measuring yourselves against a realistic set of numbers. Otherwise, it can become demotivating to the point that you don't take your own numbers seriously anymore and start operating in the dark. The process also has another upside: it takes into account the team's input, who will then feel accountable for the numbers they fed into.

   Start by developing a **strategic vision** over a 3-year perspective, before you then break this down into targets for the year ahead. You will inevitably have competing strategic directions, and with limited resources you won't be able to undertake them all. Should you open up China or tackle B2B? The closer you get to seeing the finishing line, the more you will look at short-term impact. In order to compare apples with pears, every initiative has to be put forward with a detailed business case. This should provide answers to the amount of investment and resources needed for what output, to determine the Return on Investment (ROI). It's all about getting answers as to where each person's effort and every euro should be invested. In the end the highest ROI should win.

2. The **budgeting forecast** puts plan-numbers behind each initiative on both the cost and the profit side. If you create Profit and Loss statements (P&L) like that for

each business unit, this makes the business more manageable and holds the P&L owner accountable. It's a trade-off, in which the finance department rightly tries to stretch their budget, while the owner of the initiative will often come up with objectives which are too conservative or even pessimistic. Challenge them to set their bar higher! You need to be ambitious, as you will only reach the targets you set yourselves!

Once the forecast is agreed, the finance team has the challenge of creating an overall budget that can be funded and can bring the desired output at the same time. In tech-heavy environments, you can invest in new technologies that support your growth for more than a year, channeling your spending through capital expenditure (Capex), which makes your balance sheet look great and is attractive to investors.

You need to appreciate that the whole budget is based on estimated guesses. The best budgets I have seen baked in wildly unpredictable external factors like terrorism, countries leaving the EU, elections of populists, strikes, natural disasters and power outages. The way to do this is to leave some room to wiggle. What usually happens is that one strategic area ends up delivering better than another. This is not an issue as long as each area can be counter-subsidised, so that you achieve your overall budget targets in the end. But even the best planning in the world reaches its limits when none of the initiatives have worked as planned, like in the years of the global pandemic.

You will get better and more efficient at this process over the years. By the time the finish-line is in sight, you will be able to prove that you have become true financial experts. This will gain you extra credibility with potential acquirers and will be reflected in your valuation price.

3. Once the budget is in place and the new financial year starts, you need to track on a regular basis where you stand against the plan. That's where **controlling teams bring in reporting**. Just like for HR and other processes, try to automate this as much as you can, or scaling your monitoring will become like chasing windmills.

    The controlling teams should see themselves as a service centre. In reality, with results and financial numbers becoming more and more the heart of the operation, the finance teams become increasingly in charge of the show. That changes the whole dynamic of the company, but you should still insist on transparency and support to the teams, especially in finding solutions when roadblocks appear. At the same time, it's also the finance team's duty to step on people's feet to receive an explanation on budget deltas and to ensure that immediate counter actions are being taken.

Ideally, you should show real-time data on dashboards across all the offices, to make it easy for teams to follow. If you don't bring your teams on this journey with you because your tools fail you, the entire planning process will have not been worth much.

4. With each month that has passed since the start of your financial year, you will get a clearer view on where you will come out in the end. If you become aware that your assumptions are completely off, **a transparent and immediate reforcast is required** to ensure that you continue to track realistic numbers. That doesn't release you from the overall annual business targets though. What may be taken away from one area of the business needs to be added to another one, reallocating resources with it. I have also seen circumstances that have led to plans being corrected upwards. For example, when Iceland's famous volcano Eyjafjallajökull erupted in 2010, all flights were suspended and consequently this brought more traffic to the railways than we had ever anticipated at the time. Just from one day to the next, my target went up by 10%.

Extending your runway

While KPIs and budgeting are becoming more important as a sign of maturity and are key assets to get to an exit, there is still nothing more important than having sufficient cash in the bank at the end of each month. And although, you should be spending all your money to prove that you're able to scale without reaching a ceiling, there is a fine (bank) balance which needs to be achieved. Your number one KPI for yourselves must be to always have just about enough money in the bank to be able to continue your journey. That is why the rest of this chapter will talk about the **4 ways to extend your runway in a scale-up**:

1. **Decrease costs**
2. **Internal growth**
3. **External growth**
4. **External funding**

Now, ideally you can combine all four, and while you should look at growing, and at reducing unnecessary costs and expenses at all times anyway, making an acquisition or raising additional funds will require heavy resources that can take your focus off the business and therefore should be rare events.

1. **Decrease costs**

    Decreasing costs and reducing expenses can be seen as standing in opposition to full throttle growth, but this is not necessarily the case. You should always be mindful of your costs. I have seen numerous cases where companies have neglected to look at their costs during a period of rapid growth. Then the next round of fundraising has not gone as planned, as it almost never does, and suddenly they have been forced to reduce their costs heavily just to survive. So, don't let things get to that point before you start to **constantly question your cost base**. Do you really need that specific subscription, and can you renegotiate better rates for your software licence? Question everything (within reason) and hustle for the best rates. Scrutinise your travel expenses, logistics and fulfilment costs as well as exploring the possibility of outsourcing some of your second level operations.

    By the way, the best way to learn about where you can reduce costs is to ask your teams. I have seen them be particularly creative when it comes to this exercise. Just make sure that you don't waste their time or scare them unnecessarily. But the message is clear: controlling costs is crucial, even during the euphoric moments of strong growth. Everyone should consider it part of their role to never stop looking at ways of ensuring that every euro is spent wisely.

2. **Internal growth**

    Given that you have found a profitable business case to operate on, growing your sales and revenues inhouse is the most obvious approach to ensuring a long run of liquidity that allows you to spend and grow from within. And while I have covered this topic in previous chapters, there is one angle that I have not shed light on yet, which is **monetising your product to increase your take rate**. Just be mindful that this often doesn't play well with early adopters and team members. It may be that you have always marketed your product/service as a clean, no frills UX which focuses solely on what you do best. And yet, here I come suggesting, for example, that you cross-sell insurance onto your rental car platform to commercialise your product.

    So, this becomes a delicate balance. On the one hand, you are in a phase where potential acquirers are taking an interest as to whether you are able to add ancillary products or services and make them work commercially. This is to help them to assess how much value your business could add to theirs after a potential acquisition. On the other hand, at this point you don't even know if there will be an exit, and you don't want to compromise your product, jeopardise your identity or lose focus while blazing new trails. Therefore, if you go down this route, test and make it as light as possible in a way that adds clear value to your customers.

3. **External growth**

It might sound like a contradiction to suggest that **an acquisition or a joint venture could increase your liquidity**, but these can in fact be great ways to achieve this. Let me explain – from a business perspective, everything starts with a classic make-or-buy decision. If you feel that there is something that somebody else can do better than you, ideally at a better price and can still help to generate additional revenue, then explore this opportunity. And an option to explore could be that any acquisition is (at least in part) funded through debt.

This is especially the case when two companies together can leverage more negotiating power than each of them would alone, while also increasing their joint valuation. A good example is when Trainline acquired Captain Train. Both respectively were about to enter each other's markets with a similar approach and product. Trainline was strong in the UK market and now wanted to build a European business. They could have committed to significant investment inhouse to achieve this, but it would have taken them a huge amount of time to obtain the necessary expertise and put the right licences in place. Acquiring Captain Train, with their knowledge and expertise in the European market, was therefore a perfect fit. Not only did it shorten the development time drastically, it also removed a potential competitor to the UK market. So, when resources and time are critical and assets and markets are complementary, acquisitions or joint ventures are definitely something to consider.

4. **External funding**

Last but not least, there is what every start- and scale-upper goes through multiple times in the lifecycle of their company: fundraising. As a scale-up closer to an exit, you will probably have gone through at least these three rounds across the previous few years: There will have been, as a start point, some seed investment. Then, usually doubling or tripling in value each time there will have been an A- and then a B-series, probably with a gap of a couple of years between each round. The sums of money typically involved in each have changed dramatically over the past 5 years. In 2014, when we raised €5M in the B-series for Captain Train, we made it onto the front page of several big newspapers. Today, a €50M series would not even raise a mention in the same press.

However, regardless of the zeros in the sums, the question remains whether it is necessary to go into a C- or even a D-series or whether you would want to try to exit before this or whether you can **find other ways to finance the business without embarking on more funding rounds**. The upsides of conducting another round are potentially to be able to scale further and achieve a much higher valuation. However, in my view this can come at a high risk. Firstly, your portion of the company will reduce significantly. Secondly, you need to be aware that with every €50M more added to the valuation, your exit options become more limited. And thirdly, only the large funds have the financial means to invest at this point. This will come with the price tag of needing to give them at least a couple of board seats, and they will demand significant involvement in your business, which will change your everyday life forever. And, is it worth the huge amount of time and effort needed at this stage to raise money? You will be removed from the organisation for several months just at the time when you're needed the most.

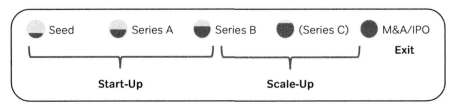

Fig 20: *Typical Start- then Scale-up fundraising cycle until an exit*

So, taking all of that into account, my recommendation is that if you want to raise another round at this stage, make sure that your company is set up in a way that your COO can run the business without you. Either way, it is crucial to be able to continue to scale and grow to now be best prepared for the final chapter of your great adventure.

TOP 3
Takeaways

1. Choose the right KPIs to track your progress

2. Take budgeting and monitoring seriously and involve your teams

3. Make your runway a priority and consider alternatives to fundraising

CHAPTER 9

And Now, it's Really Time to Play

Your wisely selected KPIs should now prove that you know how to scale successfully and that you are capable of manoeuvring around obstacles and ceilings in your way. You are now playing in a league where you consider that it's the right time to exit. But do not pop the champagne bottle just yet. What comes now is a combination of chess play and a roller coaster ride, requiring you to keep a cool head. Until the money is in the account, anything can still happen. All your achievements could be worth nothing if you do not get the last steps right to make it over the finish line.

This is the moment to confront you with the brutal truth: while you are already exhausted by all the time and effort that you have invested over the last few years, I must tell you that it's nothing compared to what to expect on this potentially final mile of the journey. Get ready to rumble and give everything you have got this one last time to make the exit happen.

A European viewpoint

As this is a European story, it is worth talking about the climate for scale-ups and exits here, even though most exits still happen outside Europe. There are major differences between three of our main capitals, London, Paris and Berlin, when it comes to exiting scale-ups. London still hosts the most important exits and the largest numbers of unicorns. Although Brexit is not helping our British friends, I see too little systemic change in my home country, Germany, for example, to be confident that Berlin is going to catch up anytime soon. France considers itself a start-up nation and has caught up considerably, with every exit being frenetically celebrated as a symbol of national pride. And while in Berlin and Munich together, there are even more unicorns than in France, there have been very few important scale-up exits in Germany recently.

The differences are even greater on the tax side of things. Depending on your country of residence, they might eat up a large portion of the money you make. All this is completely unharmonized across the EU, which is a disaster for my beloved so-called Union. We have had cases where people have paid twice as much tax for the same deal in the same business, just because they lived in two different European countries.

However, I remain positive that the EU will harmonise further and create one economic zone, unfortunately excluding now the UK of course. This requires some serious investment, focus and commitment from politicians all over the EU. Personally, I acknowledge that I would never have concluded the successful double exit I did, if I had been based in Germany or Italy in the 2010s. I hope that in future these kinds of success stories will also be possible in other European countries, and not only between Paris and London, like it was for me. You need to pay attention to these wider geo-political considerations and watch carefully how these develop over the next few years, to factor these in as part of your exit strategy.

Why exit?

Before I talk in detail about the process of getting over the finish line, let's take a quick step back and ask: **why do you want to exit at this point?** Being clear on this will improve your sharpness in any upcoming negotiations. You can only achieve your goal when you are one hundred percent clear on what you want your output to look like. When it is only about the money, you can just accept any good offer on the table. However, after all the years of time, effort and deep involvement you have committed to this project, you can be sure that there is more than just money in it for you.

Figuring out what motivates you, will mobilise your final resources. Think of yourself as a marathon runner who is at kilometre 40, turning right for the last time and can now see the finish line for the first time. The last 2 kilometres depend not on physical strength but mental resilience. What carries the runner through these last couple of kilometres is to imagine what it must feel like to have arrived on the other side. So, what are the reasons why you are choosing to exit, and what does success after arrival look like?

- **Become rich:** What is a price that you would consider fair? Ideally, enough to allow yourself and your long-time superstar colleagues to be able to choose what comes next.

- **Be free to do what you love:** This was one I felt strongly about, being independent and free for the rest of my life. Read this chapter until the end and you will learn that an exit is hardly ever the end of the story though. But it might bring you closer to a point of more freedom, and surely that is a great motivator to make it through the next few months.

- **Be satisfied:** Do you need an exit to feel that you have brought it to an end? To me it was the logical consequence, kind of adding the roof to the house that I had built. And I remember one of the funniest and somewhat satisfying things that came with the exit being the people who had never believed in the project in the first place now trying to get close to us. It proved that we must have done something right.

- **Feel that "my baby" is in good hands:** It's your project after all, you have put your heart and soul into it and have given so many incredibly talented people a professional home. To me, finding the right exit was also about finding a safe haven for the ship that I sailed the seven seas with for all those years. And, for you personally, if you decide to stay, you wouldn't want now to have to work with people you don't appreciate either. Make sure your exit is a cultural fit with a company that ideally is complementary and adds something that you do not yet have, to be even more successful together.

Types of exit

Once you are clear on your motivation to exit, let's look at the possible **types of exits** you might choose from. The earlier you started working towards one, the more likely it is that you will have competing parties to choose from when it comes to it.

1. **M&A:** A merger with a competitor, in which your company is acquired by another market player, to be swallowed and grow stronger together. Or an acquisition by a private equity firm which believes in your growth potential and plans for a bigger exit in the future under their control, by providing you with sufficient funds, networking, and expertise. In both cases, expect to lose much of your decision-making power.

2. **IPO:** Initial public offerings are still rare in continental Europe, representing only 10% of the €200bn of the world-wide IPO value in 2019, according to PWC's IPO watch. The upside is that you can continue to operate your business relatively independently. The downside is that this represents a huge investment and taking risks beyond your control to get there. Prepare to endure permanent shareholder pressure and additional reporting burdens once the float has been successful.

3. **Personal exit:** If you leave your affairs in an orderly manner by installing a great CEO, the board might let you leave with a fair cash-out of the current valuation price and your shares vested to hold until the next exit. This can in fact sometimes even help the business, if you are no longer as motivated as you were at the beginning, or you are simply now not the right person to run the show anymore. But be careful to not have regrets looking back or it to be perceived that you are abandoning your own project too early.

These three are your main realistic options but, for full disclosure, I would like to mention three more types of exit that are hardly ever discussed, because they are less prestigious:

4. **Spin off:** You could choose to sell off the part of your company that is especially valuable, as an independent enterprise. To do so, have it freshly valued and issue new shares for this part only. This allows you to grow your capital, helping you to operate more independently and to accelerate growth. By focusing on just one part of your story, you might attract more and different investors.

5. **Liquidate:** In circumstances where you feel the business is a lost cause, you could liquidate parts or the whole of the company to save at least some assets and pay some invoices and salaries before you shut it down. Obviously, this might leave a bitter taste, but it doesn't have to – sometimes it's better to bring things to an end properly, in a managed way, rather than just let it drown by itself, slowly and painfully.

6. **No exit:** And last but not least, how about having no exit at all?! Instead, just create a strong brand and a viable, growing business like it was the objective for every company in the good old times? I know, this is not what you came into this for, but if you have found the magic key to scaling, made the business model work, and still love what you're doing, why be dogmatic and ignore this possibility?

The key thing to avoid is the recently trendy scenario of raising hundreds of millions of euros but with no working business model and no case to exit. In that situation, in the end, you have none of the above options available to you, but a huge amount of money to pay back. There are always strings attached to that cash, regardless of the euphoria of the initial investment frenzy!

The exit process

Now that you are clear on your motivation and your preferred exit type, let's dive into the process to write a **happy ending to your story, in three final acts**:

1. **Creating traction**
2. **Exit preparation**
3. **Negotiating and closing the deal**

1. Creating traction

The chances that someone just comes around, knocking on your door to acquire you at your dream price are slim. Having said that, we were lucky enough that this exact thing did happen to us, but you cannot rely on it. Once you feel ready and your numbers back up your story and your exit plan, you should proactively start to pitch your case. And this is where we also pick up on the second objective of marketing from Chapter 7: corporate communication.

Finding the right tone is a fine line. On the one hand you want it to seem like you have all the time in the world, with plenty of alternatives, and on the other hand you want to be explicit enough on the fact that you are up for sale. This requires delicate orchestration and plenty of experience, which you should leave to the experts.

What you are trying to get to, is a scenario where you can choose between a set of best options, with parties competing with each other over the price of your business. When you make it to having in place three options, you can then call this a healthy choice. The level of preparation to secure one, two or three options is in fact virtually the same.

Depending on your level of maturity, you could even go for the master class, a dual track approach. What this means is to prepare an M&A and an IPO at the same time, particularly as the preparatory work involved in part is the same. I explain the differences further on in this chapter. You can then decide on the most lucrative option at the very last minute. Whatever you choose, nothing should happen by accident. And while you may want to make it appear that the exit is just a fortuitous approach by an interested party, it requires a great deal of effort to create sufficient traction around your business where this can even start to happen. Here is how you can send potential buyers clear signals through the grapevine to get the game started:

- **Use your board members and investors** to have informal, external discussions. They will know whom to talk to, spreading the news without putting you in a needy or weak spot. This will help you to get a better flavour for the appetite in the market, as well as what they are precisely looking for, so that you can position yourself correctly.

- Depending on what kind of exit you have chosen, you can send a clear sign **by announcing an addition to your board with respected experience** in that specific exit type.

- Among your top USPs, **showcase the ones that meet current market trends**. For example, these could be demographic changes, digitisation, liberalisation, climate change or even the fallout from a pandemic. Personally, I was surprised how much of the hype depended on our story hitting the zeitgeist. It's all about timing, and often, a bit of luck.

- **Continuously increase your external corporate communication**. Start to add KPI figures now and show off that your numbers are now underlining your story. Demonstrate you are now ready. Also, give more interviews on key topics, to position yourselves as a thought leader and expert in what you do.

- You need some big last-minute victories, without risking a blow-up. Having invested in **lobbying** before, allows you now to be more aggressive and accelerate this, without being in the firing line yourself.

All this is an iterative process, where you will constantly increase your understanding about how you are being perceived. And with every discussion you have, you will become better at focusing on the one thing that stands out for your interested parties. But no matter how well you manage this situation, you will need to exercise patience. I have seen exit projects that were perfectly well-managed be derailed close to the exit. All sorts of factors can come into play, some within your control and others the result of random external events: the incoming offers might be too low, a terrorist attack suddenly changes the whole dynamic, or the role of the new CEO couldn't be agreed on. Let's be clear, this is not the exception, but the rule: at least half of the time, it doesn't work out.

What is important is not to panic! You need to make sure that you have a stable, properly functioning company in place throughout this process that you can go back to if needed.

And therefore, while you are aiming at creating tension externally, you need to have in place the opposite internally. With all the transparency in the world, do not inform or involve your teams too early, as this only creates friction and takes the focus off the important day-to-day stuff of running a successful business. Confidentiality is key until everything is signed. As an insurance policy, in case there is a leak, you should prepare internal and external statements saying that nothing is going on. Even when your teams might have sensitive antennae that pick up that something is happening, this is not the time to be entirely open with them. Your working assumption still needs to be that it's not going to work out, but if it does, they will learn about it and understand early enough. I had a good laugh when we tried to be discrete and asked our bankers to come to the offices, dressed more casually to avoid unnecessary questions. So, they took their ties off and replaced their jackets with black pullovers – all of them. We obviously didn't have any incoming questions when twenty men, all dressed exactly the same, came to offices full of people in t-shirts. *rolling eyes smiley*.

2. Exit preparation

When interested parties start talking about you and enter discussions with you directly, you need to be ready to promote your business and yourself in the most professional and elaborate way possible. This requires meticulous and detailed preparation work. I will start with the generic elements applying to all types, before I focus later in this chapter on the two most common exit types, the M&A and the IPO, with the latter requiring a specific type of prep work.

The most important thing is to understand that an exit, unlike fundraising, cannot be managed by the CEO alone with just a small finance team in support. The finance and legal teams now officially need to take over, throwing everything they have got at this one. In fact, it will require input from many teams, which makes it even more challenging to not bring the business to a standstill. The COO ideally entirely runs the business at this stage, and only a few key and hand-selected confidential people should be involved in your preparation work. Other than legal, finance and the C-suite, this team usually consists of the chief of staff, the HR head, as well as a few specialists from the tech, product and ops teams. And if you ever wanted to feel like James Bond, this is the moment, as every exit project will have a suitable code name so that you can refer to it without others becoming suspicious. It can be your favourite city or the name of your pet. Your creativity knows no limits but try to align the name with the interested parties or it can become confusing.

This inner circle team will need to sign NDAs to be able to freely share all relevant information, but also to ensure that it stays there. I have not even spoken to my family about most of these exit discussions. For outsiders it is impossible to judge how important confidentiality is, so I didn't want to put them in a situation where they might mention it to others without being aware of the harm this could cause to the process.

And when it comes to the big exits, especially an IPO, you will also need to bring in external superstars to support your prep work: banks, financial advisors, your investors and other board members with their experience from former exits are valuable here. If you want to make it a great success, you will need the crème de la crème, with your counterparts being professional sharks who have done this a hundred times and know how to use all the tricks in their favour.

You will find yourself in legal and financial depths beyond your imagination. I will never forget having to keep rereading my first 120-page shareholder agreement, trying to understand my obligations and my rights. I felt like the most stupid person in the whole world and had to trust for the most part in the counsel we onboarded for that reason. Over time, you will get more used to reading these kinds of documents.

Now that you have your team in place, it is important to define roles, tasks and deadlines. The combination of not being able to share with anyone why you are quasi disappearing, having to pretend at work that nothing is going on, combined with tremendous pressure and a lack of sleep over weeks and months, will push your limits beyond what you ever thought was bearable for you. In my professional career, I had been used to crazy working hours, had regularly early starts at 4 in the morning to travel to several countries a week over a period of a decade. But all this was nothing compared to what I experienced during these exit preparation times. That's why I say that you need understanding loved ones. And bear in mind the risk that it could all end up being particularly frustrating, with you having invested all that time, effort and stress, and yet it might still not work out, or it could get delayed.

Your only option is to get into a tunnel. One where you might not even see the light at the end for quite a while – you just need to function, and only retrospectively ask yourself how you made it through. You will make it, and I hope that it will be worth it. One thing is for sure: the better prepared you are, the higher your chances of success. People only see the success on the visible part of the iceberg, but not the effort underneath the surface to get there. The same goes for me – while people notice the successful M&A and IPO, they don't notice that I have been involved in several deals that haven't worked out. It's just that, obviously, nobody speaks about those failed deals.

When you wake up the morning after a potential deal that you have worked on day and night for months and find that it has been called off, you need a huge amount of inbuilt motivation to pick yourself up, dust yourself down and get back to your real life and start again. I have always allowed myself a day at the sea, on my own, when this has happened, just to take stock and gather my thoughts and my energy again. I have then been able to get back to it again, like nothing had ever happened. You need to look at the plus side, because your time has not been wasted: your decks, documentation and numbers are ready now, and you have gathered experience that will reduce future stress and help you to plan and anticipate things better for the next round.

Alongside a great team, you need to put in place the things I have described in this book up to this point and then you should be all set. All those properly implemented procedures, and the detailed documentation you have put in place, will have brought up your valuation. I have seen a case in Paris where the preparation and documentation were so well done, and the story so amazingly well sold, that it added a double digit million number to the price. Therefore, starting early and preparing for this day saves hassle and adds value at the same time. Once you have left the start-up phase and have entered the scale-up zone, you should start immediately on indirectly always preparing for the exit moment.

And it's that preparation and experience that will also help you later in your negotiation phase, so let's fast-forward for a second to the point where you have agreed on the pillars. Then, you need to be prepared for an avalanche breaking lose, which goes by the name of Due Diligence (DD). What this means, in a nutshell, is that you will be asked to open your books and answer a million questions on all your internal processes and numbers, to check that your story holds up. As this will require a huge amount of extra work, I recommend that you start preparing for this as early possible, even though it will only come into play later in the process.

Here is how to get started: Everything you need to share should be entered into a data room that you provide selective access to. All that counts are data points here: what you can't prove, you can't claim. Your greatest story is now not worth a cent if your data doesn't back up every element of it. And the better your internal processes, documentation and tracking tools have worked over the past few years, the easier it is at this stage to extract the necessary information to get the highest possible confirmed valuation. This is also the moment where you can show off your marketing and product playbooks you have worked so hard on. Other than that, here are the **top-10-elements that you will need to prepare for your DD**:

Finance/ Business
- Detailed business case with a 3-year forecast
- Current and next year's budget
- KPIs and tracking tools

Market
- Size of the opportunity: how big is the market, what is your share, market trends, competitor analysis. You will need to provide detailed sources for all this.

People
- Have the key team members present themselves and their departments, using great-looking charts
- The organisational chart as well as key JDs and working contracts
- Hiring plans

Product & Tech
- Are your platform and your product compliant with all rules and regulations and are there any potential technical or security risks (fraud)?

Legal
- Corporate governance: are you respecting compliance and ethical rules, human rights protection laws, labour laws, data protection (GDPR), etc., and do you sufficiently document this and train your staff?
- Supplier contracts: is there anything in there that could be a potential limitation to growth?

By this stage at the latest, also make sure that all share plans are signed by your teams, to avoid chaos when it comes to it. My experience is that people do not take the whole share thing seriously enough, because it remains at that point hypothetical. As they are inevitably not fully aware of the big picture, you need to double-check this on their behalf.

3. Negotiate to close the deal

You are now perfectly prepared and feel ready to enter the negotiation phase to secure the deal. But heads-up, so much can still happen until you get there. There are still serious discussions and eventually contracting processes to be gone through. From someone who went through an M&A and IPO process within 3 years, I say to you: agreeing in general is one thing, getting to a deal on paper that all parties feel comfortable signing is a whole different story.

Before we dive into processes and negotiation points, let's just quickly remind ourselves of what we are trying to achieve here. We are aiming at getting to the highest possible price. The goal is to **maximize your valuation (formula)**, which (unless you have positive EBITDA) reads roughly:

Valuation = Annual Revenue * X

(X: depends on your industry and your future potential)

Regarding the annual revenue part of the formula, your only chance for negotiation is to arguably use your run-rate or your sales numbers instead of your current revenues. Whatever you decide on in the end, it needs to be a tangible number from your balance sheet. Defining the X-factor, the multiple that will be applied to the revenues on the other side, leaves you room for interpretation, and that's where your persona and your skills and powers of persuasion come in. With all the data points in the world, this bit is about credibly selling your dream, based on a personal interaction between human beings. Potential buyers want to get a feel for you, your team and the market. They need to believe that it's worth the hassle to go through a DD. Show them what they want to see: that the graph goes to the top right, how big the market size is, explain that your portion is still very small, but provide a clear plan to owning large chunks of it in the future. Elaborate on current trends and benchmark your business, and all the beautiful things you could do with more money. However, even the best story will not change the fact that the multiple range is inevitably limited by the industry and the markets you are operating in. Transportation and travel tech were leading that race for a while, but now medical biotech, fintech and other sectors are catching up, with double digit multiples while I'm writing this.

We agree that the price is the first key element to negotiate, but what are the other **important terms and conditions of your deal**, and how can you best negotiate them? My best piece of advice is to never come across as being under pressure or being dependent on this deal. Those facing you on the other side of the table will use all their negotiating training and game strategies to get you where they want you. Don't let them put you in a corner. On top of your own wellbeing, you are negotiating on behalf of your entire team, who are not even aware of what's going on yet. It's a huge responsibility that will decide so many people's financial futures as well as their job security. And most importantly, it's your baby in which you have invested so much. It's hard to put a price tag on this, and it's hard to let go, so it is essential that you feel comfortable with the deal.

But whilst thinking about the company and others is a noble thing to do, you shouldn't forget to stand up for your personal interests, because nobody else will. So, what is it that you personally want out of this deal? Do you want to stay, or do you want to leave as quickly as possible? At this point, it's not wise to be transparent about your potential plans to leave, as the price of the company may well depend in part on your commitment to stay invested. Your new owner might even put in place a lock-up clause for a couple of years to hinder you from leaving. So, if you are staying, at least for now, regardless of whether you want to or are being forced to, negotiate more influence and more new shares to make the next part of the adventure worth its while for you.

To help you to get an overview of the other elements you should consider in your negotiation, here is **my top 3 list of the terms and conditions that I negotiated** following my plan to stay in the company:

1. **Mitigate your personal risk.** There will be terms governing the cash-out portion you can take versus the amount you are obliged to leave in place as a roll-over (the portion of shares you have to leave invested in the new company). You should aim for your **cash-out portion to be around 50%**, although even for an IPO that would be quite high. When you are committed to stay in the company and believe in their continued success you can try to roll-over more, but my advice is to mitigate the risk and make it 50/50 if you can. You should also negotiate a 'kicker'. This is when the value of your shares become exponentially higher when you exit above a certain price.

2. **Agree on the shape and your impact of any joint project.** If it is a merger, what is each company in charge of after the deal, and will you keep the brand and the platform? What is the plan of how the team size overall and in each office is going to develop over time? **Negotiate your position, job title and reporting line as high up as possible.** Get a seat on the group board, with voting rights.

3. **Negotiate your lock-up period** on two elements: Firstly, when are your **shares fully vested** until? This is usually until the next exit or one year after an IPO. And in case your plan is to leave before, it is important to agree on the exact definition of being a "good leaver", so that you don't leave empty handed. Secondly, **negotiate your non-compete clause** to not be hindered to work in your industry for longer than a year, and for the settlement related to this to be worth at least 60% of your gross salary.

And while you would want to conduct all the above discussions calmly in a backroom somewhere where nobody else can hear you, I promise you that it will leak at some point, with false rumours to be expected, and all this will put you in the spotlight. Sometimes these leaks are even intentionally floated by the potential buyer to put additional pressure on you. Just be mindful that whenever you think the pressure couldn't get worse, something else will come up. And that's exactly where they want you. At this point you need to get back into the driver's seat and take back control of the wheel, to get potential buyers bidding against each other to drive up the price. The greatest thing I heard in one negotiation I was involved in was, "Hey man, surely we're not going to fight over €10M!?" For someone like me, who comes from a background where €100 is good money and not a piece of paper to light up your cigar, this was a key moment. I knew that we were now moving in the right direction when the price went up by €10M in an instant. There can be a lot of money and responsibility involved, but you need to see it for what it is: a game. Only when everything is signed or the bell at the stock exchange rings, should you inform your wider teams. At this moment you then need to provide them with as much information as possible before they learn it from the press.

The M&A and IPO processes step by step

Now that we understand what to negotiate for, let's look in greater detail at the steps for the two biggest exit types you're most likely to choose from.

The M&A

1. **Start discussions:** You will have personal discussions to get to know each other, build trust, to find out whether there is a cultural fit and if you can agree on a complementary project that adds value to both sides. You will **show presentations** and have a run-through of all key departments and numbers that allow a potential buyer to put together a first case. When you go out of these discussions with a good feeling and see potential, you should definitely continue.

2. **Sign the terms:** Then roughly agree on the terms and conditions of a potential deal, check in with the board on whether to proceed and sign a term sheet. It is worth investing a fair amount of time into the negotiation of this document. The clearer and more transparent you are with each other at this stage, the smoother it will become later, pending that the super-well-prepared DD from above will confirm all the assumptions. If this is not the case, and queries and complications emerge, the time between signing the term sheet and getting to the final signature under the purchase agreement can be more than half a year. If the M&A then fails, it has not only eaten up huge amounts of your time and energy, but it might have put your business as a whole at risk.

Be aware that delaying tactics are common, designed to put you in a weaker position, with decreasing liquidity. Be mindful that your competitors might abuse this process just to look at your books for obvious reasons and without any serious plans to merge. In the case of known competitors reaching out to you, there is a need to play safe and not share anything that could give them a strategic advantage. Therefore, it's good practice to include some penalties to prevent this, and add non-disclosure elements to ensure your confidentiality as much as possible. Ideally, there should not be more than a few weeks between signing the term sheet and the end of the DD to confirm its modalities. And then you need to look each other in the eyes and either go for it or stop, to not waste any more time.

3. **Sign the deal:** If you then agree on the final terms, you need to involve even more external legal people to get the paper war set up and, in the end, pending the final confirmation from the board, sign shareholder (purchase) agreements and capitalization (cap) tables.

4. **Close the deal:** The actual closing a couple of weeks later is a purely legal formality, and only then will you receive your money. Ideally, from point one up to the conclusion of closing the deal should only take a couple of months. More realistically, for mature scale-ups with big money involved, it can take many more months, which, if you can, I strongly discourage you from letting happen.

The IPO

The reason to do an IPO, besides bringing in fresh money, is to find a steady home *and* continue to operate almost independently. However, the process to get there can be complex, risky and costly, which is one of the reasons that they are still fairly rare in Europe.

Let me outline the backdrop to the IPO that I was involved in. In 2019, the year Trainline achieved one of the top 10 European IPOs of the year, Europe saw a 40% decrease in listings vs. 2018, according to PWC's IPO Watch. So, how did we still manage to float despite complicated markets and its timing being in the middle of the Brexit discussions? It all comes down to exhaustive prep-work and good decision trees to anticipate all possible outcomes. You need to accept that some things are just beyond your control and could derail your best efforts, even at the last minute. All you can do, when you have a strong business, is significantly increase your chances by properly **preparing and executing your IPO**, following these 5 steps:

1. **Make the right choices:** Choose a stock market in a country where you have considerable business, or you might be perceived as trying to hide something.

Gauge the right timing that anticipates as best as possible all external factors (elections, etc.).

2. **Prepare thoroughly:** Allow at least six months of preparation: sometimes, in fact, a good starting point is when you have already prepared your material for a prior exit plan that didn't work out. Be aware that the preparation of the prospectus, the roadshow material and registration documents require even more time than for an M&A.

3. **Conduct roadshows:** These will seem endless, with little sleep and an unhealthy lifestyle. Also, say goodbye to your family and friends for a while. During the first roadshow, you will speak to investors to see how many subscriptions you could close, to get a first feeling for the demand and the price of the shares you could go public with. Ideally, you have managed to book everything twice during this roadshow. By the way, this is not only a roadshow, but also a road trip which takes months and will make you travel across the globe. The second roadshow will take place just before the actual listing. Your goal is to place all shares that will be floated. The price range will evolve during the discussions, and the exact amount of money raised will only be determined once the share price is set.

4. **Declare an intention to float:** Over a few weeks, every day, the C-team will have to confirm that they are not aware of any changes to what has been communicated in the prospectus on which basis the IPO is planned. Only then can you fill in and submit the official intention to float with your stock exchange of choice and with whom you obviously have been in contact for a while now. At this stage you can expect communication to leak. Don't comment yet.

5. **Go public:** two weeks after the submission of your intention to float, you go ahead with it. You have fixed the price and you are now going public with the share part you decided on and are raising significant liquid funds to continue to grow heavily. Even at this point, between the intention to float and going public, still around half of the deals don't happen.

You have closed the deal!

And with this right mindset, you will manage to close the deal and maybe stand on a balcony yourself one day, like we did in 2019 at the London Stock Exchange. Your story will trend on Twitter, and that's when you start realising what has just happened: you did it, the exit is not near, it's here, and you're finally allowed to pop the champagne.

(Image courtesy of The London Stock Exchange, https://www.lseg.com)

And once all the pressure has fallen away and the money is finally in your bank account, this does something to you. You experience that amazing feeling that you have brought it successfully to an end. You will party for a couple of days, and with the adrenalin ebbing away, months of inhuman pressure will lift from your chest, and then two interesting things happen. Firstly, anybody who has ever been involved in an exit then begins to understand the value of their shares and how this will change the way you look at things forever. Secondly, success is attractive, and even your haters now want to be friends with you. My highlight was a top industry CEO who would never receive us before, inviting himself to our offices to see what we could do together after our merger with Trainline. And that's why it's important to remember who was there for you before, because success can fade again, and you want to surround yourself with real friends. In a nutshell, be proud of your amazing achievement, but stay grounded, because from now on you will be taken seriously and the time of the challenger has officially come to an end.

Your next chapter

But this is not the end really. Take it all in and enjoy yourself while you can, because shortly you will realize that after the exit, is really just the beginning of a new chapter, with new challenges ahead. This is one that is not discussed enough, even though it will again consume a huge amount of your energy.

After a merger, when the smaller company is to be integrated into the bigger one, a lengthy complex process starts that once more requires all your energy. This is **the Post Merger Integration.** Your deal came at a price: you're locked in for a while and have less independence and decision-making power now that you are part of a larger group, and so you need to work out your position in this new setting. The way you proceed, as a role model in that procedure, will determine how others will follow. I have seen entrepreneurs being overwhelmed by the more corporate-like decision-making processes they are now confronted with, where previously they could simply decide alone. And like yourself, your entire team is struggling to understand their places, while you are having to bring together two cultures of two businesses and often even different countries. What makes this even more challenging is the need to let go of what is globally seen as the weaker brand or less-used product that people have built and put their heart into. When you know this needs to happen, the best way is to get it over with as quickly as possible. It will be short and painful, but then you can move on and invest your energy on more fun topics such as winning new customers and markets together. However, be prepared to lose some of your great people in that process. They have been around for longer and have made good money in the deal, but it shortly might just not be the same company anymore that they loved so much. When they are crucial for the business, try to keep them as long as you can, but even then, when they start being disruptive to the business and a threat to the culture, let them go. It really is OK – you had a great time together.

When you have concluded an IPO, the time following this will mostly be around understanding **how you are expected to behave in a public listed company**. Confidentiality increases, to avoid insider knowledge getting into the wrong hands even internally, and substantial quarterly reporting must be published. Commercial life now has become more about short-term growth and permanently pleasing your shareholders. What I also hadn't realised before an IPO was that there are more recurring roadshows to be done after your listing. They may be a bit shorter in duration but will still take a fair bit of time out of your agenda.

But no matter what type of exit it is going to be for you, on one aspect you should work hard to turn the clock backwards: legal and finance, who have taken over the company to get it to the exit, want to continue to run the company, enjoying their newly gained power.

I have spotted this phenomenon in large corporates as well as in scale-ups, regardless of whether the deal was closed or failed. As much as it was important to have them in the lead during the final few months before the exit, it is now crucial to go back to having them operate as service functions, and to put the business units and P&L owners back in charge of running the show. Otherwise, legal and finance will become constant showstoppers to innovation and speed.

And with this said, I hope you all find yourselves with that incredible feeling of having succeeded in smiling disbelief when looking at your bank account statement one day soon. If you have made it to here, it's a great achievement and I salute you for your success. Make sure it was worth the hassle and use everything you have learned and earned to make you happy. And just like I was asked to at times, pass on to others what you have learned along the way, to give them guidance for their success.

TOP 3
Takeaways

1. Be clear on your reason to exit

2. Choose the right exit type and create traction

3. Keep a clear head until the very end

APPENDIX

Your Playbook Summary

Section I: The Foundation	
Before You Start	Does the business have a clear set of values and goals, and do you share them?
	Does the company have a solid foundation to grow on?
	Is there a (hidden) roof that could hinder a successful scaling process?
The Early Scaler	Create as much content as early as possible
	Decide on your brand and stick to it
	To be able to scale, avoid niche-dependent IT solutions
The Corporate Athlete	Be very mindful of your energy levels
	Make time to think
	Focus on your time management
Section II: The Scaling Phase	
HR	Hire an HR head and start documenting and thinking in organisational structures
	Put your culture at the heart of everything you do, and develop your high potentials
	Set up a working recruiting and onboarding process that allows you to move fast and let go asap of people that become poison for the culture
CEO	Develop a vision and a leadership style that make your team want to follow you
	Focus on where you can add the most value as a CEO
	Successful leaders surround themselves with external thinking partners
Product & Tech	Build one flexible, reliable and secure platform
	Start your product thinking from the end and improve your funnel
	Use your data to test, scale and anticipate the future in the best possible way

Marketing & Comms	Identify your USPs to build a clear story for your business and branding
	Be clear on whether your communication is consumer- or corporate-facing
	Continue to use all organic channels extensively and add paid channels to generate more demand while keeping your customers engaged
Section III: The Exit Preparation	
Finance & Admin	Choose the right KPIs to track your progress
	Take budgeting and monitoring seriously and involve your teams
	Make your runway a priority and consider alternatives to fundraising
The Exit	Be clear on your reason to exit
	Choose the right exit type and create traction
	Keep a clear head until the very end

Glossary

Or how you win at bullshit bingo

ARR – Annual Receiving Revenues

ATV – Average Transaction Value

BC – Business Case

B2B – Business to Business

B2C – Business to Consumer

C-Level/ C-Suite – CEO or his direct reports/ job titles starting with C for Chief

CAC – Customer Acquisition Costs

CLV – Customer Lifetime Value

CPA – Cost Per Acquisition

CRM – Customer Relationship Management

CCO – Chief Commercial Officer

CMO – Chief Marketing Officer

COO – Chief Operating Officer

CPO – Chief Product Officer

CRO – Chief Revenue Officer

DD – Due Diligence

EA/ PA – Executive/ Personal Assistance

EBIT(DA) – Earnings before Interest, Taxes, Depreciation, and Amortization

GDPR – General Data Protection Regulation

GMV – Gross Merchandise Volume

IPO – Initial Public Offering

KPI – Key Performance Indicators

M&A – Merger & Acquisition

MAU – Monthly Active Users

MUU – Monthly Unique Users

NDA – Non-Disclosure Agreement

NED – Non-Executive Director

OKR – Objectives and Key Results

P&L – Profit & Loss Statement

PPC – Pay Per Click

PSP – Payment Service Provider

RACI – Responsible, Accountable, Consulted and Informed

ROI – Return on Investment

SaaS – Software as a Service

SEO – Search Engine Optimisation

USP – Unique Selling Proposition

VC – Venture Capital

Bibliography

Kline, N. (1999), *Time to Think; Listening to Ignite the Human Mind*, Ward Lock / Cassell: London.

Loehr J, Schwarz T. (2011), *The Making of a Corporate Athlete*. Harvard Business Review.

Lencioni, P. (2002), *The Five Dysfunctions of a Team*, Jossey-Bass: San Francisco.

PricewaterhouseCoopers LLP (2020), PWC IPO Watch Europe 2019, London.

Printed in Great Britain
by Amazon

22827414R00090